T0055150

THE POLITICS OF CHAOS
IN THE MIDDLE EAST

The CERI Series in Comparative Politics
and International Studies
Series editor CHRISTOPHE JAFFRELOT

This series consists of translations of noteworthy publications in the social sciences emanating from the foremost French research centre in international studies, the Paris-based Centre d'Etudes et de Recherches Internationales (CERI), part of Sciences Po and associated with the CNRS (Centre National de la Recherche Scientifique).

The focus of the series is the transformation of politics and society by transnational and domestic factors—globalisation, migration and the postbipolar balance of power on the one hand, and ethnicity and religion on the other. States are more permeable to external influence than ever before and this phenomenon is accelerating processes of social and political change the world over. In seeking to understand and interpret these transformations, this series gives priority to social trends from below as much as the interventions of state and non-state actors.

Founded in 1952, CERI has fifty full-time fellows drawn from different disciplines conducting research on comparative political analysis, international relations, regionalism, transnational flows, political sociology, political economy and on individual states.

Olivier Roy

The Politics of Chaos
in the Middle East

Translated from the French by
Ros Schwartz

Columbia University Press
New York

In Association with the Centre d'Etudes et de
Recherches Internationales, Paris

Columbia University Press
Publishers Since 1893
New York

Library of Congress Cataloging-in-Publication Data

Roy, Olivier, 1949–
   [Croissant et le chaos. English]
   The politics of chaos in the Middle East / Olivier Roy ; translated from the French by Ros
Schwartz.
      p. cm.
   Includes bibliographical references and index.
   ISBN 978-0-231-70032-0 (cloth : alk. paper)
   1. Middle East—Politics and government—21st century. 2. United States—Politics
and government—2001– 3. Middle East—Foreign relations—United States. 4. United
States—Foreign relations—Middle East. 5. Islam and politics—Middle East. 6. War on
Terrorism, 2001– 7. Iraq War, 2003– 8. World politics. I. Title.

   DS63.1.R6913 2008
   956.05'4—dc22
                                        2007044187

∞
Columbia University Press books are printed on permanent and durable acid-free paper.
This book is printed on paper with recycled content.
Printed in India

c 10 9 8 7 6 5 4 3 2 1

INTRODUCTION
THE WAR ON TERROR: BETWEEN WORLD WAR IV AND OPTICAL ILLUSION

On the night of September 11, 2001, with American public opinion whipped up to a frenzy, the United States government had carte blanche. It was determined to punish the guilty and prevent a repeat of what was the first attack on home soil since 1812: and people were prepared to pay the price, whatever the human and financial cost. The rest of the world was either supportive or silent, prepared either to join a coalition led by America or to bow to the anger of the superpower which had been wounded and offended, but was at the pinnacle of its power.

Six years on, the failure is patent: none of America's objectives has been achieved. Bin Laden is still alive in 2008, and so is the Taliban leader, Mullah Omar. Even their putative deaths would not put an end to the movements they control. Terrorist attacks have not ceased, and the situation throughout the entire Muslim world has deteriorated. Far worse, it is Washington's bitterest enemy, Iran, that has gained the most from this new situation, which is likely to lead to further confrontations. Presented as the precondition for the eradication of the causes of terrorism, military intervention in Iraq has proved to be a fiasco, which has played into the hands of America's designated enemies, i.e. Iran and Al-Qaeda. The American army's intervention capability is now stretched to the limit, while divisions and new alliances are proliferating in the Muslim world. The Taliban are back in Afghanistan, while in Lebanon, Hezbollah makes no secret of its determination to make or break any government in Beirut. The Islamist militia in Somalia could only be defeated by an Ethiopian military intervention, which is tantamount to making the Islamists the defenders of the nation and thus paving the way for their return to the political arena. Those in power in Baghdad are Shia and sympathetic to Iran. Hamas is the dominant political force among the Palestinians. Iran is pursuing a nuclear programme which at best would only be slowed down by an aerial bombardment whose consequences would be burdensome for the United States to manage. And finally, America no longer appears to be the hyperpower in a unipolar world, but a power tied up in knots, incapable of policing the world. It must forge new compromises with its allies and with rivals whose credibility is growing steadily—China, and even Russia.

How did it come to this? It is neither the resurgence of the Taliban, nor Al-Qaeda's pugnacity, nor the determination of the Iranians which put the Americans in such a hopeless situation. This failure emanates from Washington. The Bush administration's strategy was based on two major errors: firstly, conceiving of the retaliation for 9/11 as a "global war on terrorism", and secondly, making the military intervention in Iraq the linchpin of this new strategy. These two decisions are the result of an ideological vision of international relations developed within the neoconservative group that also includes the more traditional Republicans like Donald Rumsfeld and Dick Cheney.[1]

But while it is fitting to blame the arrogance and incompetence of the Bush administration, the ideas that drove the American neoconservatives are still part of the current climate, muddying the traditional left/right divide. In effect the neoconservatives claim they have a duty to carry out a

---

[1] As I pointed out in *Les Illusions du 11 septembre* (Seuil, 2002), the neoconservatives should not be confused with their allies on the Christian right.

humanitarian intervention. They broke, albeit temporarily, with the old Western policy of support for authoritarian and nepotistic Third-World authoritarian regimes, which were assumed to be pro-Western, and guarantors of enforced secularisation. They spoke of democratisation and freedom. They did not demonise the Islamist movements—at least not at first. They praised civil societies and reform. The neoconservatives pushed to extremes the idea that Western values are universal and must be promoted, through direct intervention if need be; in this sense, they are closer to a left-wing progressivism that rejects cultural relativism of any kind than to a colonialism anxious above all to maintain the prevailing order.

Contrary to expectations, the global controversy over the American intervention in Iraq did not set the European pragmatic realists against the dogmatic American ideologues. In actual fact, everywhere in the world the debate was based on great ideas, prejudices and ideological references. In France, political figures from the left, such as Bernard Kouchner, found themselves in the same camp as the American neoconservatives with a policy that pushes the concept of the "duty to intervene" to its logical conclusion. The term was coined twenty years earlier in condemnation of the major powers' indifference to the fate of peoples whose human rights were being trampled on. The Third-Worldist, anti-American left, on the other hand, found itself on the defensive, forced to deny there was any validity in the neoconservative line which they claimed spoke of freedom solely to guarantee US oil interests. It is this left that has ended up supporting highly undemocratic movements (from Cuba to the Taliban and even Saddam Hussein) claiming that they represent sovereignty and the fight against imperialism. The Third-Worldist left stresses the fact that American policy is essentially neoliberal, promoting the privatisation and globalisation of the economy, but this same left is unable to come up with an alternative other than supporting profoundly authoritarian movements. Champions of sovereignty of all hues (including President Chirac) claimed the humanitarian intervention in Iraq conflicted with international law, in defence not of democracy but of national interest, and more generally, the idea that the world depends on there being a balance of power and not on a utopian concept of international justice and law. Lastly, left and right alike are both deeply divided over their attitude to Islamism. The identity-focused Christian right, just like a left that is more secular than libertarian and more Republican than Democrat, willingly supported the concept of fighting against the Islamic threat.[2] The words "crusade" and "jihad" are brandished, while there is fresh talk of the "free world" confronting the "forces of evil". Inevitably, examination of the repercussions of 9/11 and the subsequent debate on the line to take on terrorism raise the question of Islam. Social issues are more closely bound up with strategic debates than ever before, which probably explains the popularity of "clash of civilisations" theories as well as references to World War IV and "Islamofascism". But this globalisation of the threat makes any rational strategy impossible and paves the way for a hollow, bombastic rhetoric, which above all serves Western societies' internal debates. The problem of immigration and Islam in the West is externalised by projecting it onto the Middle East, which obeys a different logic.

The Israeli-Palestinian conflict is central to this debate: is it the main cause of the Middle East crises and of Islamic radicalisation, or is it just one conflict among many? Should the priority for diplomatic action be to resolve this conflict, or will it gradually die down as the other tensions are defused? Or does it have a logic of its own that separates it from the other issues, like the tensions between the

2 On the debate in France, see Olivier Roy, *Secularism Confronts Islam*, Columbia University Press, 2007.

Basques and the Spanish? Whatever the answer, it is clear that the mere reference to this conflict makes it possible to articulate more general questions on the Middle East: for example, the question of the relationship between anti-Zionism and anti-Semitism and its implications for the way the debate progresses.[3] The Middle East becomes the stage for the European debate on "multi-culturalism" where European anxieties are reflected.

Analysis of the evolution of the various Middle East crises cannot be divorced from a discussion of the major concepts of society being bandied about today, from Islamism and terrorism to democracy, civil society, multiculturalism, etc. The aim of this book is to relocate the conflicts of the Middle East in their own context, while attempting to understand how they are related to the major issues facing Western societies. In short, it is a matter of demolishing the idea that there is a "geostrategy of Islam" that would explain all the present conflicts, from Palestine to Bin Laden to the riots in the Paris suburbs.

Far from bearing out the prevailing theory that there is a "clash of civilisations" and a confrontation between the Muslim world and the West, the conflicts and realignments

3   See Pascal Boniface, *Est-il permis de critiquer Israël ?*, Robert Laffont, 2003.

affect primarily the Muslim world itself and operate along fault lines that have very little to do with ideology. In contrast to the "old refusal front"—namely those states and movements that traditionally refuse to accept or acknowledge Israel—that unites Islamism and Arab nationalism against Israel and the West, there is a growing rift between Shia and Sunni Muslims which puts the conservative Arab regimes in the same camp as Israel and could ultimately redraw the map of the Middle East.

The military intervention in Iraq has indeed resulted in a profound geostrategic transformation of the region, but along lines that go beyond the ambitions of the American decision-makers. Ordinarily, any dominant power tries to maintain the status quo, whereas the Americans destroyed it and overturned the strategic balance of the Middle East. The unipolar world that had been anticipated after the fall of the USSR did not last long: for around a decade, the Americans (including under Clinton) were able to intervene unilaterally, without worrying about their actions being endorsed by Security Council resolutions, and built temporary, bespoke coalitions involving only their allies. And then, in four years, the major power proved incapable not only of reshaping the Middle East, but also of managing local conflicts or even of making their adversaries knuckle under by simply threatening to use force. American credibility is damaged. Having armed forces that no country can hope to defeat on the battlefield is no use. The asymmetric war of the weak against the strong, illustrated by the roadside bombs in Iraq which cause the majority of American casualties, has been transplanted into the strategic domain. One can speak of an "asymmetric strategy", according to which weak states (Syria, Pakistan, North Korea, Iran) put America in a no-win situation by drawing it into an impasse or confronting it with impossible choices. The most spectacular of these is unquestionably the blackmail threat of their own obliteration: nobody wants to topple President Assad in Syria or General Musharraf in Pakistan, whereas it is an open secret that these two countries offer sanctuary or support to terrorist groups and radical movements, simply because their destruction would be worse than their current nuisance capability. "Attack me if you dare" not because I'll defeat you, but because destroying me will make things worse for you.

The United States thus finds itself paralysed just as China and Russia are seeking to assert themselves as major powers once more, using traditional instruments of domination (control of territories, energy sources and transport), which are perhaps outdated now, but which reflect a world that is once again multipolar.

Meanwhile, Al-Qaeda's terrorists are deploying in a space that is more deterritorialised and globalised than ever, thus eluding all the traditional instruments of power, which are now ineffective.

1
WHO IS THE ENEMY?
WHERE IS THE ENEMY?

Unquestionably, the United States had to react to the events of 9/11. A military intervention in Afghanistan was the obvious response, as there was no doubt that the attacks on the Pentagon and the World Trade Center were organised by members of Al-Qaeda operating from Afghanistan under the protection of the Taliban regime. The preliminary to any campaign against the terrorist organisation was therefore to deprive it of its territorial sanctuary. The aim of Operation Enduring Freedom, launched on 13 October 2001, was to destroy Al-Qaeda's bases and overthrow the Taliban. It was sanctioned by a UN consensus which the Europeans, including France, agreed to. Initially, the intervention on the ground in Afghanistan was a success.

Military operations could have ceased at that point, in favour of more classic anti-terrorist tactics using the intelligence services and the assistance of the police and judiciary in the relevant countries. At the same time, diplomatic and political action aimed at building a stable coalition between the states concerned by terrorism could have been undertaken, and relations developed with Muslim communities so as to isolate the extremists. But in launching the concept of the "global war on terror", the Bush administration had a much more sweeping plan: to eradicate terrorism, its causes had to be uprooted. At that point in time, the argument made sense and was shared by a good number of opponents of American policy. It remained of course for the "causes" to be established.

When one goes to war, the first priority is to define the enemy and the objective. To do that, the adversary must be identified, the battlefield where the confrontation will take place selected, and the available resources tailored to meet the objective (or the objective tailored to meet the resources). And finally, once the terrain is conquered, a political alternative that makes it impossible for the enemy to return must be put in place.

The first problem is that the Bush administration had already designated the main enemy prior to 9/11: Saddam

Hussein's Iraq. The battlefield would therefore be Iraqi territory, and the alternative to terrorism implied regime change in Iraq and the democratisation of the Middle East. The second problem is that the Bush administration categorically refused to acknowledge that there was no connection between Saddam Hussein's regime and international terrorism. The American army soon became mired in the conflict. From then on, Washington was on a headlong ideological collision course, defining the enemy—"international terrorism"—in terms that were increasingly woolly and ideological ("Islamofascism"), thus depriving itself of any leverage or influence over events on the ground. The last problem is that the administration was never able to tailor its resources to its objectives, either in military terms (what kind of army is required to wage war on terrorism?), or political ones (how do we promote stable, legitimate, pro-Western regimes? How do we develop a "moderate Islam"?), or even in terms of propaganda (how do we communicate our aims?).

THE OBSESSION WITH IRAQ

The American leadership's resolve to invade Iraq was only hardened by 9/11.[1] Instead of responding appropriately to

1   See *Les Illusions du 11 septembre*, *op. cit.*

the attack, it took advantage of the American public's thirst for vengeance to impose its original objective: the overthrow of Saddam Hussein. The idea went back a long way—to the early 1990s to be more specific. The neoconservatives like Paul Wolfowitz, then Deputy Secretary of State for Defense, had distanced themselves from President Bush senior in February 1991, at the end of the first Gulf War after the Iraqi army had been crushed. They opposed his decision, supported by the oil lobby and the Saudis, to call a cease-fire leaving Saddam Hussein in power. Then, during Bill Clinton's presidency (1992-2000), those same neoconservatives campaigned against the Oslo Accords and Clinton's ongoing, voluntarist involvement in negotiations between Israel and the Palestinians. They did not see the Israeli-Palestinian issue as the cause of the tensions in the Middle East; other crises had to be resolved first, and meanwhile Israel should be allowed to act as it saw fit. The main threat was Saddam's Iraq, followed by mullah-led Iran, and only the removal of existing dictatorial regimes could create the conditions for resolving the region's conflicts.

When Bush junior took office in January 2001, the neoconservatives and their allies (Donald Rumsfeld, Dick Cheney) occupied all the senior positions and thought they would at last be able to implement their strategy. But the first months of the Bush administration were taken up by tensions with China; those advocating a military operation against Saddam Hussein were champing at the bit. By the evening of September 11 however, the operation was possible. Intervention in Afghanistan was the obvious answer. It would still be necessary to convince the public and the decision-makers that this was only a prelude and that the real objective had to be Iraq, as the main threat was Saddam Hussein's regime.[2]

From the outset, the priorities were reversed and the fight against Al-Qaeda replaced by that against Saddam, or rather against Baghdad. Three arguments were necessary to legitimise this shift in objective: paint Saddam Hussein as an enemy far more dangerous than Bin Laden, which explains the hysterical campaign over weapons of mass destruction; present Bin Laden as an agent and instrument

---

2 In early November 2001 I met Paul Wolfowitz, the then Deputy Secretary of State for Defense, in Washington. The conversation focused solely on the concrete conditions of the intervention in Afghanistan (which I supported). As he showed me out, he said: "I fear however that this Afghanistan business will distract us from our true objective." "Meaning?" "Iraq, of course!" That said it all: the Americans intervened in Afghanistan purely for reasons of expediency, because Bin Laden was there. But they had no long-term vision for the Afghanistan-Pakistan-Central Asia region. This was consistent with the fact that Afghanistan had never interested Washington except negatively: against the Soviets and then against Bin Laden.

of Saddam Hussein, hence a whole disinformation campaign on the links between the two;[3] reduce Bin Laden to a secondary phenomenon, merely the expression of a more general radicalisation of the Muslim world which had to be addressed by a reshaping of Middle Eastern societies. In this scenario, intervention in Iraq was only a first step, both the easiest and the most productive in the long term. The motivations behind the manoeuvre were all the more sincere given that the American establishment never grasped the new terrorist phenomenon, systematically seeking (until 2006) to hold a state liable.

This was neither opportunism nor manipulation. The neoconservatives had forged a coherent global vision that was to a certain extent respectable, even if it were to prove disastrous, because it was ideological. Here we should be wary of traditional analyses from a section of the anti-imperialist left which sees American Middle East policy either as being defined in Tel Aviv or as governed chiefly by oil interests. In intervening in Iraq, the Bush administration was neither seeking to control oil nor acting on Israel's wishes.

---

3 A theory consistently maintained by Laurie Mylroie, for example in "The Saddam-9/11 Link Confirmed", *FrontPage Magazine*, May 11, 2004, and in *Bush vs. The Beltway: How the CIA and the State Department Tried to Stop the War on Terror*, Harper Collins, 2003.

AN ILLUSION: THE INFLUENCE OF THE OIL LOBBY IN THE DECISION TO INVADE IRAQ

The oil magnates' Texan exile

The aftermath of 9/11 saw a plethora of articles, blogs and books explaining that George W. Bush represented the interests of the American and Saudi oil lobby. But relations between the Bush camp and the Saudis were abysmal after 9/11; a neoconservative fringe even wanted to portray the Saudis as the true force behind Islamic radicalism (e.g. Stephen Schwartz, Laurent Murawiec and, outside the strict circle of neoconservatives, influential authors such as Daniel Pipes). Meanwhile, the oil lobby, embodied by the former Bush senior team, led by his former Secretary of State, James Baker, and supported by the "Arabists" in the State Department (the diplomats, often Arab speakers, involved in Middle East negotiations since the Reagan era), was opposed to intervention in Iraq. It was this team too, when in power in 1991, that had decided not to occupy Iraq territorially, at the price of maintaining Saddam in power. Having left with Bush senior, these people were not recalled to power by Bush junior in 2001, and they withdrew to the Baker Foundation, Houston (Texas), keeping their distance from the new government. They returned to the public eye with the famous Baker report, published in November 2006, which consisted of a radical, wholesale critique of the Bush junior administration's Iraq and Middle East policy. This report was loftily ignored by George W. Bush. The major American petroleum companies, such as Exxon, also remained highly circumspect, showing themselves to be critical both of sanctions against Iran and of the occupation of oil-producing areas, because they preferred stability, i.e. preserving the status quo, to the delusion of a new regional order.

In actual fact, the Iraq war changed nothing as regards the energy equation. It is sufficient to note the Americans' inability to re-establish and even less to control Iraq's oil production to realise that this was not their objective in going to war. Washington's avoidance of a policy of military control over the oil producing areas is of course not motivated by a respect for national sovereignty, but by faith in the primacy of the market over production: it is the market that sets the prices and regulates production, whereas any attempt to make it a strategic weapon, following OPEC's example, is destined to fail. There is now a clear break with the imperialist policy that prevailed in the 1950s (the ousting of Mossadegh in Iran) and advocated direct or indirect control of oil-producing areas. Today, as long as no country has a monopoly, it is the market that determines prices. So the priority is to guarantee the freedom of the market, not to take control of production. The first Gulf War can be explained partly by the determination to prevent Iraq from becoming too powerful a player on the market, as a result of its occupation of Kuwait. Once this attempt at hegemony was thwarted, there was no point controlling the oil wells. The same rationale applies to Afghanistan: a gas pipeline linking Central Asia to the Indian Ocean via Afghanistan is only of interest to the companies that built it, and for a one-off profit, not those who might operate it, since this gas will go to the only accessible market: India. It cannot be transported to Europe or America. It is worth noting that the United States' only voluntarist political intervention in the oil sphere was the promotion of the Baku-Ceyhan oil pipeline (completed in 2004), linking the Caspian Sea to the Mediterranean via Turkey and bypassing Iran and Russia: here too, the key issue was to keep the market open and fluid, not to control production. When the former head of the "Fed", Alan Greenspan, writes in his memoirs that "the Iraq war was for oil" he too is referring to the oil market, not to control of the oilfields. For oil companies, success does not depend on extending production for they are investing in refineries much less than hitherto; finally estimating reserves is not a scientific exercise but based instead on the impact that such forecasts have on prices.

Controlling the rising price of oil was never a priority for Washington, since higher prices also benefit American producers and make it possible not only for the exploration of new gas and oil fields to be profitable, but also to finance research into new energy sources, as the former CIA Director James Woolsley tirelessly points out. It is also worth noting that the vagaries of the situation in Iraq had no effect on the price of oil in the international market, which fluctuated considerably, but for completely different reasons. In January 2007, when the situation in Iraq seemed catastrophic, the price per barrel fell to below $50. Iraqi production was 3 million barrels a day before 2003; it was reduced by half in 2006, a third of which was consumed nationally. Iraq accounts for only 2% of global production and can attain 6% with the investment of $21 billion over the next decade. The return of Iraqi oil onto the market will therefore be gradual and will not be disruptive. The market price today is determined primarily by demand from India and China, and the loss of Iraqi oil has been compensated by an increase in Saudi production. In any case, the market is not affected by whether the American army controls the Iraqi oilfields or not, but it would be affected by a war between Iran and the USA, due to the disruption of transportation in the Gulf.

This does not mean that the business world is indifferent. Whereas the oil giants were noncommittal before the intervention, the service companies and civil engineering sector on the other hand were very much for it: the latter effectively fulfil their contracts in a very short space of time (six months to four years), and so are not affected by strategic ups and downs. More to the point, they are paid by the American tax payer, whereas the energy companies work on a long-term basis and seek a stable relationship with the authorities in the oil-producing countries. The oil companies are currently negotiating with the new Iraqi government to persuade it to pass a law on investment in the energy sector that would be beneficial to them. But they know all too well that such laws can be changed.

Israel: a sacrosanct ally, fiercely independent and hard-pressed

Any American Middle East policy assumes the unconditional defence of Israel, but goes beyond this imperative. And if support for Israel has been even stronger under the Bush administration than under its predecessors, it is not so much thanks to what Washington has done, but to what it has not done, in other words compelling Israel to mend fences with its neighbours, both Palestinian and Lebanese. Not putting any effort into the peace process is tantamount to allowing the Israelis free rein.

Bush's policy towards Israel has two strands. The first is once again the neoconservatives' vision, set out in a report written in 1996[4] (a report aimed in actual fact at the leader of Likud at the time, Benyamin Netanyahu), and in the publications of the Project for the New American Century think-tank, set up in 1997. It is diametrically opposed to the Oslo process and President Clinton's entire policy: Israel must have a completely free hand in order to guarantee its security and define and fulfil its strategic interests; bartering territories for peace is out of the question, the objective is to ensure armed peace. The Israelis must be allowed to do as they wish with the Palestinians, who are not yet approaching the point of giving up.[5] This leads to the second strand, specific to President Bush: his desire to

4   Richard Perle (ed.), *A Clean Break: A New Strategy for Securing the Realm*, Institute for Advanced Political and Strategic Studies, 2006.

5   "If Israel is to protect itself, it must achieve a comprehensive military victory over the Palestinians, so that the latter give up their goal of obliterating it." "The Only Solution [for Israel] is Military—I and II", Daniel Pipes, *New York Post*, Feb. 25 and April 2, 2002.

differentiate himself completely from his predecessor Bill Clinton. Bush particularly did not want to put a great deal of effort into shuttle diplomacy between the protagonists of the Israeli-Palestinian conflict.

Allowing Israel this latitude with regard to its exclusive Palestinian and Lebanese preserve does not imply that Washington concurs with Tel Aviv on other fronts. If the pro-Israel lobby in Washington (American Israel Public Affairs Committee, AIPAC) supported the intervention in Iraq, it was primarily out of a concern to back the Bush administration, considered the most favourable towards Israel, but also because it wanted to dissociate the overall question of the Middle East from the Israeli-Palestinian conflict, namely: leave Israel to deal with the Palestinians and give Washington the job of intervening in the Middle East to put an end to the terrorist threat.

Naturally, the Israelis were delighted to see the back of Saddam's regime. The neoconservatives' conviction that a democratic and therefore Shia-ruled Iraq would be pro-American was also echoed to some extent in Israel: such an Iraq would isolate Iran and catch the Sunni Arab front—both in its religious form (Salafism) and its nationalist form (pan-Arabism)—in a pincer movement. The old Israeli dream of an *alliance de revers* was taking shape again. But even so, the Israeli leadership never believed in the policy of democratising the Arab world which was at the core of the neoconservatives' project. Israel anticipated that such a policy would lead to the Islamists gaining power, whereas it preferred to negotiate with "secular" dictators whom it disliked but knew well. It also feared that the obsession with Iraq would distract the Americans from what Israel considered to be the real threat: Iran, not a coalition of Arab countries as in 1948, 1967 and 1973. For all these reasons, Israel did not push for the attack on Iraq, but nor did it oppose it. Furthermore, a number of Israeli experts feared that an American military intervention in Iraq would automatically make a potential strike against Iran's nuclear facilities impossible, either because the Americans would be bogged down in Iraq, or because the survival of their new Iraqi protégé would require Iran's neutrality. Which was spot-on, even if an attack is still possible and can change the landscape.[6] For Israel then, it is definitely Iran which is the

---

6   In February 2003, I attended a briefing given by Dan Meridor, strategic affairs advisor to Ariel Sharon's government at the time. His analysis was very clear. Below is a summary: no Arab regime, including Saddam Hussein's Iraq, poses a strategic threat to Israel; the threat is Iran, because of its nuclear programme; an American military intervention against Saddam Hussein is politically desirable because it would involve the Americans further in the Middle East, and that is good for Israel, but it is strategically risky, as it would make the Americans dependent on their relations with Iran and would limit

main threat today, especially since Hezbollah's power in Lebanon has increased.

In fact, whatever conclusions one draws from the failure of the Oslo peace process, one of its outcomes, along with the collapse of the USSR, was to transform the Israeli-Arab conflict into an Israeli-Palestinian one. Unable to aspire to any kind of strategic parity with Israel after Russian support ended, divided among themselves and beset by Islamist disputes, the Arab states all accepted Israel in their various ways, ranging from Jordan's *entente cordiale*, Egypt's cool but functional relations, an objective convergence of interests for Saudi Arabia (against Iran and Al-Qaeda) to a *modus vivendi* between cantankerous neighbours, namely the Syrian regime whose collapse was feared (lest the Islamists were to benefit). The deterioration of relations between the Israelis and the Palestinians, which resulted in the "second intifada" in 2000, thwarted the grand vision of those who supported the Oslo Accords: the emergence of a Palestinian state in economic symbiosis with Israel, which would have made it possible to integrate the Jewish state into a sort of Middle East common market whose overall economic development would have curbed various types of nationalism and radicalism. But the failure of Oslo has

---

their strike capability against the Islamic Republic.

resulted in Israel becoming more cut off from the "Greater Middle East" than ever. Israel's strategic ambition has been reduced to that of a bastion, defended by a wall, confronting a Palestinian (and south Lebanese) glacis which is neutralised by sporadic attacks, with anarchy gradually setting in. This is considered preferable by Tel Aviv to the order embodied by a state in the hands of a democratically-elected Hamas.

And so Iraq was not even a central preoccupation for Israel, which was fully preoccupied with a close enemy (a Hezbollah-Hamas axis) supported by a distant enemy with a nuclear potential, Iran. Tel Aviv would like to see an American attack on Iran, but believes it should only rely on itself, given the uncertainties surrounding American policy for the coming years. This augurs for unilateral initiatives in the context of an Israeli leadership crisis, which will not contribute to the region's stability. Effectively, the latitude given to Israel has led to a deterioration of the situation. In prioritising security over finding a political solution and in allowing the settlements to continue without an overall plan, Israel has routinely undermined any Palestinian authority and has never allowed the conditions to emerge that would enable a Palestinian government to be stable, credible and reliable, thus vindicating the most radical elements on both sides. Officially, most Israelis and Palestinians and the international community support the two-state solution; the problem is that the conditions on the ground now make the creation of a viable Palestinian state impossible.

What then motivated the American decision to invade Iraq, apart from the simple wish to "finish the job" with regard to the Gulf War? A coherent ideological project, encapsulated in the "Greater Middle East" (GME) programme.

THE GREATER MIDDLE EAST REFORM PROJECT

Like the American electorate, the Bush administration is not homogeneous. There are numerous fissures between the Christian right, neoconservatives, pragmatists, isolationists and interventionist Republicans (like Rumsfeld). At the start of his first term, Bush took a unilateralist and relatively isolationist line: the United States would only intervene occasionally to defend its strategic interests. He rejected the key concepts which were the basis for international action in the 1990s: no state-building, no more nation-building, no investment in the peace process. His defence minister, Donald Rumsfeld, embarked on an overhaul of the American army with the aim of streamlining it and gearing it for short-term operations, which could be on a massive scale, but based on the shock and awe tactic, where the emphasis is on technology, fire power and special forces—a far cry from the build-up of ground troops and heavy tanks witnessed during the first Gulf War. Long-term occupations, counter-insurgency campaigns and far-reaching political action were out of the question. In the event of a conflict, the aim would be the wholesale and rapid annihilation of the enemy. In short, such an instrument is precisely the opposite of what the current situation in Iraq requires, even if it did fulfil its role perfectly in the strictly military campaign that culminated in the overthrow of Saddam Hussein.[7]

After 9/11, the neoconservative team was the only one to put forward a "constructive" programme that was compatible with the President and Rumsfeld's views. The military campaign, expected to be short, would be followed by a

---

7   It was not very hard to understand that the issue was not the military campaign, but the ensuing occupation. In the wake of the US intervention, I wrote: "Washington has claimed that it can create a friendly, democratic and stable Iraq within two years. Forget it: achieve two of those adjectives and consider yourselves lucky. There is no democracy without nationalism, and the Iraqis will sooner or later challenge the American presence. The United States cannot stand alone when dealing with the driving force in the Middle East. This is neither Islamism nor the appetite for democracy, but simply nationalism, whether it comes in the guise of democracy, secular totalitarianism or Islamic fervor." ("Europe will not be fooled again", *New York Times*, May 13 2003). I was rather optimistic: Washington is apparently unable to achieve even one of the three goals.

brief period of full occupation, modelled on that of Germany and Japan in 1945, designed to enable the Iraqi people to make the transition to democracy and elect a government that would then take charge of the country and adopt a pro-American policy, based on the people's gratitude to the United States for having liberated them from dictatorship. The agenda was definitely to bring about regime change, but without a lasting occupation. The only real long-term commitment was financial, along the lines of the Marshall plan of the late 1940s. Thus the analogy with the post-1945 era is far-reaching and explains how the Bush administration came to liken the global threat to Nazism and Communism. This is not the place to dwell on the mistakes made in the management of the occupation, in particular under the Coalition Provisional Authority led by Paul Bremer; that has already been done by several American authors.[8] We will however analyse the conceptual premises of this policy, which go way beyond the Iraqi situation.

The neoconservatives immediately ruled out any Western responsibility for the root causes of radical Islamic violence. In their view, the source of this violence is the Arab societies' institutional structures which are hindering

---

8   See in particular Thomas E. Ricks, *Fiasco. The American Military Adventure in Iraq*, The Penguin Press, 2006.

human, political and economic development. Hence they embraced the Arab Human Development Report produced by the United Nations Development Programme (UNDP) in 2002 under the authorship of the Egyptian, Nader Fergany, which highlighted the areas where there was lack of progress (literacy, publishing, Internet penetration, women's rights, etc.), and attributed it to structural causes, both political and cultural. It is worth noting that the second report by the same team (2005), which incorporated the political grievances of the populations concerned, was, on the other hand, ignored by Washington.

For the neoconservative lobby, the structural explanation of terrorism argues that it is spawned by poor "governance" of the Muslim countries in general, and of Arab ones in particular. This inability to reform is embodied by the "rogue states" like Saddam's Iraq and the Iran of the mullahs, which instrumentalise terrorism and Islamism and accumulate weapons of mass destruction in order to fulfil their ambitions. Reforming the Muslim countries was therefore at the heart of the neoconservatives' anti-terrorist strategy. They do not have a negative view of Islam, or at least did not initially. Their policy is diametrically opposed to Huntington's "clash of civilisations" theory. Here they are in agreement with the left which wants to eradicate terrorism by addressing its social and political root causes, except that for the neoconservatives these do not include the impact of American policy. They share with the left a faith in grassroots movements and a distrust of ruling elites, which coincides with their objective of cutting state bureaucracy. They also defend the concept of civil society, which for them is based on enterprising individuals and democratic personalities, rather than on collective movements. They are universalists and think that political values such as democracy can be shared by everyone. They are interventionist and advocate the duty to intervene developed in left-leaning political circles.

Far from embodying a reactionary, conservative tradition therefore, the neoconservatives borrow a great deal from left-wing reformist thinking and capitalise on a militant universalism specific to the 1970s and 1980s. This development ideology is central, for it summarises the entire evolution of the humanitarian question since the birth of the concept of the "duty to intervene" for humanitarian purposes. The main difference between the left and the neoconservatives is that for the latter, democracy implies the full acceptance of the principles of the market economy, and therefore of privatisation. As well as refusing to take the political causes of terrorism into account, the neoconservatives differ from Third-Worldist activists in their definition of "civil" actors. For the Third-Worldists, these actors are collective (peoples, classes, women, communities, minorities, political movements etc.). Obsessed with anti-Americanism, the Third-Worldists paradoxically end up defending authoritarian states and even populist dictators or leaders at the expense of democracy, which then becomes a "right-wing" slogan with the individual citizen taking precedence over a collective belonging. For the neoconservatives and the entire "sustainable development" movement, the actor is the individual. They are anti-totalitarian, but consider that democracy is based on the virtues of individualism and of the market. Their refusal to take into account the collective dimension results in neglecting the importance of cultural sentiments, above all, with the sense of national belonging and religious identities which re-emerge in regional opposition to the Greater Middle East project. And so they are also anti-culturalist, which is where they diverge from their mentor on the Middle East, Bernard Lewis, who never believed that a sudden democratisation of Arab societies was possible, aligning himself instead with realists like Kissinger and Israeli experts.

The Greater Middle East: a textbook example of development theory

From 2006, Washington relegated its democratisation ambitions to the background after the failure of the Iraqi operation. It would be mistaken to conclude that the neoconservatives' vision was simply a hare-brained scheme that fizzled out. The philosophy underpinning it is still the doctrine of the major development institutions (from the United Nations to the European Union and the World Bank). The NGOs support it under pressure from the donors, or share an anti-globalisation vision which does however have a certain number of concepts in common with the major development agencies (distrust of existing governments, encouragement of civil society, the development of microprojects, the central importance of women's and gender issues, advocacy of the humanitarian approach), while disagreeing with them over the issue of the market economy, privatisation and the relationship between the individual and society.

The GME philosophy can be summed up as follows: a democratic society based not on the state but on enterprising individual citizens removed from the web of nepotistic, tribalist and ethnic networks, operating within the framework of a market economy and practising religion as the expression of personal faith and not in allegiance to a community. The state is not an instrument of development, even less that of a political construction process; it is a regulator after the event, accountable to its citizens (all the more so as they are the taxpayers). This philosophy, inspired by John Locke and liberal in every sense of the word, underpins American political thinking and has permeated the programmes of the major international institutions since the mid-1990s (for example the World Bank, particularly after the arrival of James Wolfensohn, who was briefly replaced by Paul Wolfowitz in 2006). This doctrine has therefore reclaimed the concept of civil society as a society outside the state and even against it. It has three pillars: civil society, privatisation and good governance, and belongs to a universalist, Wilsonian and anti-culturalist, and therefore anti-Huntingtonian, view.

This doctrine was developed in the 1990s not so much by the think-tanks as by the Foundations (Ford, Carnegie), often with funding from the State Department. It gave rise to vast research programmes, including the *Civil Society in the Middle East* series of books financed by the Ford Foundation and edited by Augustus Richard Norton (even though he is the bane of the neoconservatives because he is critical of unconditional American support for Israel). The doctrine's aim is to identify factors likely to trigger a democratisation process from within (but based on "universal", and therefore American, ethical and political values). Most aid and development programmes include a "women's development" component, promoting individual betterment (women entrepreneurs, women politicians). A number of programmes stipulate that there must be a quota of women or initiatives benefiting women: for example, the development programmes implemented in Afghanistan demand equal representation of men and women on the village committees that decide on how aid will be distributed (a degree of equality that does not exist in any Western society, apart from Norway). Interestingly, this echoes the spirit of the Soviet project to transform Central Asia in the 1930s: in the absence of a proletariat, only women can be the agents of social change.[9]

This social engineering aim assumes a pedagogical voluntarism that often seems somewhat naive. A plethora of democracy and human rights training programmes and women's education schemes have been put in place. The Ford Foundation has established a centre in Cairo to launch the programme concretely (supporting in particular

---

9 Gregory J. Massell, *The Surrogate Proletariat: Moslem Women and Revolutionary Strategies in Soviet Central Asia, 1919-1929*, Princeton University Press, 1974.

the Ibn Khaldun Center under the directorship of Professor Saad Eddin Ibrahim). Volunteers and young managers from Western NGOs, often left-wingers, devote themselves to implementing programmes whose philosophy in fact derives directly from this new development theory. There are also echoes of an ethos specific to a number of Communist regimes: young activists from the cities—and the bourgeoisie—go to the country to explain liberation and the new world to the elderly and the peasants. The idea is that DIY democracy can be built from nothing: once stripped of all ideology, the "other" is putty that can be re-modelled.

Democratisation is also a market

The civil society philosophy has become the doctrine of NGOs working to promote political development and democratisation, not so much because of their members' convictions but more due to market forces: humanitarian action (apart from food and medical aid) is today essentially financed through American Congress-voted funding (this was already the case before the launch of the GME project), and by Brussels. Only the NGOs that promote development by fostering "democratisation" and civil society have access to funding. This is an important dynamic in the spread of political thinking, which is much more effective than all the propaganda that followed 9/11: the clampdown on Voice of America, the creation of a Public Diplomacy section within the State Department, the setting up of US government-funded Arabic-speaking Radio Sawa and Farsi-speaking Radio Farda, and the Al-Hurra TV station in Iraq which broadcasts in Arabic, designed to counter Al Jazeera.

But the GME also creates an internal market in the target countries. The launch of a civil society development programme has pernicious effects that have not yet been analysed in detail. But what we have been able to observe in Central Asia applies to the Middle East.[10]

"Civil society" is very often an artificial construct which has little impact, other than a harmful one, on society itself. Civil society is first and foremost a market: the sums of money brought into play destabilise the balance of microcosms (particularly that of the university), because its actors are placed directly on the market, with no state intervention. This leads to an internal brain-drain. The most brilliant academics and even entrepreneurs become involved in the programme. When a bilingual taxi driver in Afghanistan or Tajikistan earns twenty times the salary of a university professor, the most competent leave academia to become taxi drivers. In

10 Olivier Roy, " 'Civil' Society in Central Asia and the 'Greater Middle East'", *International Affairs*, RIIA, vol. 81, no. 5, Oct. 2005.

Egypt, university professors can double or triple their salary by becoming involved in a "democratisation" project: they produce reports, travel and organise colloquiums, arousing the envy of their colleagues who are less proficient in English or in the art of writing reports. Thus the actors of civil society are ostracised by their less fortunate peers, who end up endorsing authoritarian governments—which explains why, when Saad-Eddin Ibrahim was sentenced to seven years in prison in Cairo in 2000 for having received subsidies from Washington, there was almost no protest in intellectual circles, despite their criticism of the regime. At the same time, democratic intellectuals leave the local universities to go and earn a better living elsewhere thanks to democratisation programmes. Civil society tends to become a sort of artificial reservoir for an endangered species: the democratic intellectual, protected by the international institutions (Amnesty, Reporters Without Borders, State Department, etc.). Furthermore, many of them go on to leave the country and join these same international organisations.

And lastly, the privatisation policy has pernicious effects: during the mandate of the Coalition Provisional Authority in Iraq headed by Paul Bremer (2003-4), the American advisors seconded to the Ministry of Education were experts on university privatisation, which of course only intensified the disintegration of the institutions concerned. As when the Communist system collapsed, privatisation went hand in hand with widespread corruption.

THE FAILURE OF TOP-DOWN DEMOCRATISATION

And yet, democratisation certainly reflects popular demand, as is evident in people's eagerness to vote, even when the elections take place in dangerous conditions (Afghanistan in October 2004, Iraq in January 2005). Why then, is there talk of failure? Fundamentally because, for the neoconservatives and international institutions alike, democracy is a simple question of building institutions and electoral mechanisms (this also applies to the construction of Europe from the vantage point of Brussels). Building is an end in itself; it alone defines a political arena. And so Washington expected the American troops, after a tough but brief campaign, to be welcomed with rice and flowers.[11] It was thought that within two or three years, the Afghan and Iraqi peoples

---

11 During the twelve months prior to the Iraq intervention, I attended at least ten meetings with senior American officials. They always repeated the same thing: "You French, you have no idea what you're missing out on in refusing to join the coalition. We're going to be the liberators of the Arab world, the region is going to be utterly transformed, democracy will spread and you'll be out of the picture—in short: sidelined."

would establish viable democracies and robust institutions. The economy, rid of state shackles, would experience an unprecedented boom. Envious of Iraq's development, other peoples—Iranian, Syrian, Palestinian and Saudi—would oust their incumbent regimes, or at least seek reforms. The democracies would not fight each other, they would all recognise Israel, whose security would be guaranteed by the democratisation of the Arab countries. Terrorism would no longer be an option. The domino theory would operate for the benefit of the West. It is striking to see the extent to which the neoconservatives were hamstrung by historical analogies: the reconstruction of Germany and Japan in 1945, the collapse of the Soviet empire, attributed to Ronald Reagan's roll-back policy, in which, incidentally, many of today's neoconservatives were instrumental.

By explaining the problems of the Middle East as cultural or social obstacles that should be disregarded or circumvented, the political dimension of these issues and in particular everything related to United States policy is ignored, such as resentment of US regional control and its passivity in the Israeli-Palestinian conflict. But the key point that is forgotten is that there can be no democracy without political legitimacy. Now political legitimacy presupposes that the actors are deeply rooted in a country's history, traditions and social fabric, and it is here that one encounters a gap between "civil society" as it is imagined by the democratisation theorists and real-life society.

What is lacking in this theory of democratisation is the entire political dimension of a modern society (state), and the entire anthropological depth of a traditional society. The fundamental question is that of the political legitimacy of the actors suddenly placed centre stage to embody this new democracy, like the Iraqi Ahmed Chalabi. According to the civil society doctrine, it is sufficient that the actors represent this civil society for them to be *ipso facto* legitimate; but most of the time, they are perceived by the local population either as a new type of businessman, or as agents "of American imperialism and Zionism". On the other hand, while the West sees them as "new men", they very often have their family, tribal, ethnic and community connections and their own political aims, without which they would in fact be nothing.

The democratisation policy has not been altogether ineffectual. It has helped open up the political arena and allowed a certain number of political forces to have a voice and grow stronger. It should not be surprising that this applies above all to Islamist movements, since they are based on the two pillars of political legitimacy in the region: na-

41

tionalism and Islam. The Americans' (and Europeans') big mistake was to conceive of democratisation in the abstract, without anchoring it in political legitimacy.

The other issue is that of the state: while regimes are hated everywhere, the state is not. The societies of the Middle East remain torn between community affinities and statism, and consider, rightly or wrongly, that only the state can supersede community loyalties. The importance of the state is even more pronounced in the oil-producing countries (Iraq, Saudi Arabia, Iran, Algeria), for only the state can distribute oil revenues and it is hard to see how they can be privatised. This is in fact an obstacle to the development of a meritocratic entrepreneurial class, the basis for democracy, according to the GME project. In other words, it is not possible to bypass the state, and therefore internal reform of the state is required, but this reform must be conceived in political rather than technocratic terms.

A third point relates to Islam: anthropology provides an implicit lexicon of political solidarity groups while Islam provides the explicit discourse for Islamist parties to overcome social and tribal segmentation. How is democracy to be introduced into societies where tribal and clan identity is central and where people vote for the group's candidate rather than for a political programme? The Afghan and

Somali parliaments thus represent not so much political parties as gatherings of notables, whose rivalries paralyse politics and can degenerate into civil war. But this anthropological dimension is either ignored, or seen as a hindrance. The problem is to develop a democratisation policy rooted in society's anthropological reality. But there is a switch from one to the other without making a connection: one minute elections are being organised as if the political scene were made up of structured parties presenting government programmes, the next there is reversion to a policy of co-opting local leaders who receive various favours in exchange for their allegiance, as employed by the British in southern Iraq. In short, a democratisation policy carried out in this fashion does not make it possible to establish genuine political institutions within a traditional society. In both Somalia and Afghanistan, it is the neofundamentalists, the Taliban and Islamic courts, that have proposed a way of overcoming tribal and clan conflicts by calling for *sharia* (Islamic law). It is noteworthy that the neofundamentalists (those who make *sharia* the cornerstone of society) are successful in tribal and rural areas (among the Pakistani and Afghan Pushtuns, in Somalia, even in Yemen), whereas the Islamists (i.e. those who see Islam as a political ideology) have done better in the cities. But in both cases, it is the

43

arguments based on Islam that have been the most successful in surmounting clan and clientelist divisions.

However, combating these radicals in the name of secularism or a "liberal Islam" would only make sense if the
alternative actors had credibility, which is rarely the case,
at least for the time being. The *a priori* rejection of political
Islam is utterly illusory, all the more so since, as we have
long been aware, the rallying cry in the Middle East today
is "Islamo-nationalism". *Sharia* is often sought for purely
political reasons (in opposition to the Western model).

In fact, the key issue is that of nationalism: no reform
will succeed if it is not part of a national, even nationalist
vision. But the American project is clearly aimed against
nationalism. The Palestinians were ordered by the Bush
administration to democratise their society as a pre-condi-
tion to being granted a state; the underlying idea is that a
democratic Palestine would be closer to a democratic Israel
because they share the same values. It is in this illusion
that the GME's most obvious limitations lie. The problem
for the Palestinians is that this injunction to democratise
goes hand in hand with growing Israeli pressure over land
(the security wall, checkpoints, the annexation of East Jerusalem, pressure from settlers in the West Bank) and a
forceful response (raids, arrests, targeted assassinations),

even in withdrawal situations (for example the withdrawal from Gaza). On the other hand, the Israelis, Americans and Europeans did everything they could, in practice if not in law, to "nullify" the results of the 2006 Palestinian elections which resulted in a win for Hamas. Without getting into the petty game of who started it, and who is responsible for the failure of the Oslo Accords (for which the Palestinians, and above all their political leaders, also have a large share of the responsibility), the Bush administration's injunction to introduce democracy and reform before any political demands would be taken into account appears to be a way of avoiding the territorial, and therefore the national, issue.

The position of Ayatollah Sistani, the spiritual leader of the Iraqi Shia who supported the elections in Iraq and brought forward the date, summarises the weakness of the GME in a nutshell: yes to democracy, but we must defend the nation and Islam. However he himself has fallen silent since Iraq began sliding towards civil war.

Ultimately, the democratisation policy has not found the right instruments or interlocutors. True, the American diplomatic machine has tried to promote democracy: meetings with the opposition, defence of human rights, invitations, colloquia, etc., but here too the contradiction is quite obvious. For example, at a conference on

"Islam and Democracy" organised in April 2005 by the University of California, the organisers (including myself) had invited among others Nadia Yacine, daughter of the leader of the Moroccan Islamist organisation Al Adl Wal Ihsan, and Tariq Ramadan, a European Muslim intellectual. The former not only obtained her visa without any difficulty, but also received VIP treatment at the American Embassy in Rabat (which earned the ambassador the wrath of the Palace), while the latter was refused a visa by the Department of Homeland Security. Without embarking on a subtle analysis of their respective positions, it is clear that this is an arbitrary and random distinction: one is welcomed under the banner of "democratisation" and the other rejected under that of the "war on terror". This is not an isolated incident: the war on terror, waged with bureaucratic and police tactics, is contradictory to a policy of democratisation and respect for human rights, without being any the more effective, as is illustrated by the Guantanamo Bay detention camp.

This same contradiction is visible in the behaviour of the army on the ground, where it acts outside any political framework of democratisation. For example, in Afghanistan, the US army has subcontracted much of the fighting to local warlords while the embassy attempts to establish political parties. In Iraq, US soldiers fired on a demonstration in Falluja in April 2003 because they didn't see before them newly liberated citizens but enemies, thus in one fell swoop making the gulf between Sunnis and Americans unbreachable and marking the start of armed opposition. The overdevelopment and bureaucratisation of the military in the United States have had pernicious consequences: the inability of the American military to carry out a political war, where the objective is not to destroy the enemy but to rebuild a country politically; the unsuitability of its combat methods, equipment and training for a low-intensity war; and its inability to find legitimate political interlocutors in the societies where it is deployed.

Often, these failings are due to ideological prejudices: the army was not prepared for a long counter-insurgent campaign because the main threat was held to be the regime of Saddam Hussein, the ruling tyrant, backed by a powerful army, who ruled a people who wanted nothing more than to be liberated by an external force. From this standpoint, it was necessary to deploy considerable fire power in an intensive one-off operation to destroy an enemy declared a threat to world peace; then it would be possible to withdraw, once victory was secured. The jubilant Iraqi people, grateful to America for having liberated them, would rapidly take their destiny in hand and establish a democracy and the rule of law, making them the envy of all the neighbouring countries. But once again, the American army was incapable of delivering the "after-strike service", particularly as the plan for Iraq's reconstruction failed.

THE RETURN TO A POLICY OF CURBING OR ERADICATING ISLAMISM

The failure of the democratisation policy ushered in a false alternative: the return to realpolitik based on negotiation and the balance of power between states, irrespective of the ruling regime (this was the drift of the Baker Report of November 2006); and a redefinition of a global ideological foe within the ongoing "war on terror", which this time would be Islamism, even Islam itself. After the neoconservatives' failure, the battle is now between "realists" and "eradicators". They both agree on the need to prop up existing authoritarian regimes, but for different reasons. The realists consider that ideologies in fact mask national interests or simple power stratagems. In the long term, no ideology is capable of superseding national or ethnic allegiances, so one must fight and/or negotiate according to strategic interests and the balance of power on the ground. Democratisation rings hollow, not because people refuse democracy, but because it is not exportable. Several well-known neoconservatives like John Bolton, the former ambassador to the UN, have ended up moving towards this form of realism. Conversely, for the anti-Islamists, from both the right, like Daniel Pipes, and from the left, like the British Labour MP, Denis MacShane (see his op-ed in *The Daily Telegraph* on 3 July 2007), there is no such thing as a moderate Islamist.

Realists and eradicators therefore concur in advocating support for secular authoritarian regimes and are opposed to any democratic opening that would provide a gateway to power for the Islamists, echoing their refusal to acknowledge Hamas as the winner of the 2006 Palestinian elections. But the eradicators go further in urging the destruction of Islamism, depicting it as the latest ideology to threaten Western values. In a number of his speeches in 2006, President Bush mentioned "Islamic fascism", while upholding the concept of war against "global terrorism" and refusing to negotiate with regimes or organisations classed as "terrorist" by the State Department. The terms "Islamism", "Islamic radicalism", "terrorism" and "fundamentalism" (and, in France, the word "*intégrisme*") are used more or less interchangeably, and always with the implication that there is something particular about Islam, something in the religion that makes it more prone to fomenting violence.

To reiterate the point made at the beginning of this book, in order to fight an enemy, it is essential first to identify that enemy and to adopt an appropriate strategy. The more or less deliberate muddling of the above terms is precisely what makes it impossible to define a global strategy and explains two things: the very virulent and heated nature of the debate, which is always vague and sometimes hysterical, and furthermore the inability to take concrete action in the absence of a clear policy stating the various imperatives that define the Western values to be defended (freedom, integration, security and identity).

The question then is whether the role of Islam and the Middle East conflicts can be analysed in geostrategic terms.

In the ideological vision of the "eradicators" and devotees of the "clash of civilisations" theory, the "Islamic threat" has four separate but interrelated components, even if they are usually presented in a muddled way:

— terrorists—a military vanguard that undermines the pillars of the West through targeted attacks, placing more emphasis on symbols than on material destruction;

— Islamists, who campaign for a political entity (Islamic state, caliphate);

— "fundamentalists" (those I refer to as the neofundamentalists), who want to establish *sharia* law;

— "cultural" Muslims who advocate multiculturalism or community identity and who, even if they are not violent, pave the way for the first three (by defending the wearing of the veil, for example).

These four components are generally confused under the label of Islamists, radicals or fundamentalists. Depending on the whim of the writer, figures as different as Bin Laden, the Al-Qaeda leader, the European intellectual Tariq Ramadan, Tayyip Erdogan, Prime Minister of Turkey and Sheikh Yusuf Al-Qaradawi, the theologian close to the Muslim Brotherhood, are all lumped together. This makes Muslims in Europe look like a potential fifth column.

I maintain that even if there is some overlap and interference, these four components contradict each other, develop in different arenas, are based on aporiae, can only flourish in unstable systems and reflect a transition and a tension between deterritorialisation and deculturation on the one hand, and reterritorialisation and acculturation (in other words Westernisation for Muslims living in the West) on the other.[12]

Nor does Al-Qaeda's recruitment map mirror conflicts in the Middle East, since there is a predominance of young, second-generation European Muslims and converts, but there are no Palestinians or Afghans and very few recruits from the Middle East. The Islamists, like the Arab Muslim Brotherhood, are not involved in international terrorism. Nor do neofundamentalists recruit in traditional milieus, but instead among migrants, refugees, the second generation, the new social classes, or among tribes undergoing social change. Finally, the recourse to multiculturalism, far from signifying the importation of foreign cultures, in fact reveals an attempt to re-forge an ethnic and religious community in a Western context upon which has been imposed *de facto* secularisation and deculturation.

Linking these four aspects as if they comprised a global strategic phenomenon results in the inability to manage them as concrete situations. And ultimately, if Islam in Europe is becoming radicalised in various ways, this is due much more to globalisation and deculturation than to its diasporic nature, in other words its links with its cultures and countries of origin.

---

12 See Olivier Roy, *Globalised Islam*, *op. cit.*

Terrorism

The expression "international terrorism" means nothing in strategic terms. In declaring out-and-out war on terrorism, the Bush administration made it a moral category, defined as absolute evil and divorced from any social, strategic or quite simply political context. There is apparently nothing to understand, since to understand would already be to excuse (a notion that features in debates around juvenile delinquency). Of course, security and defence departments flout this moral prohibition and spend tens of millions of dollars trying to comprehend it (understandably!).

The problem of how to define terrorism remains, but to resolve it, the geostrategic rather than the legal dimension needs to be considered. From the legal (and moral) point of view, terrorism can be defined as any deliberate attack against innocent civilians in order to put pressure on a government or a society; this definition can for example act as a basis for prosecuting the individuals involved. However, on the political and geostrategic levels, such a definition is insufficient: the purpose of terrorism must be taken into account. We are now dealing with two forms of terrorism: the kind which is part of a national movement (as was the case of the Irish Republican Army (IRA) and today the Basque ETA movement, the Palestinians and the Chechens), and

53

the kind which is unfurling in a globalised, deterritori-alised space (Al-Qaeda). The first category belongs to a precise territorial framework (generally the same for both protagonists), and has clearly defined political objectives: to obtain a state and a territory. Here, terrorism is a means and not an end. Both sides commit acts of violence, even if the context in which it is exercised is not the same, hence the never-ending debate over the term "state terrorism" (if one accepts the term, the very concept of terrorism gives way to an undifferentiated political violence, where the only criterion of "justice" is that of the legal framework within which it is executed). Unacceptable means and objectives (which are generally counter-productive) for the state and target society (for example wiping the state of Israel off the map, even in the soft form of ending Israel's identity as a Jewish state), do not prevent the two from operating in the same arena and fighting for the same thing: territory, nation and state. Negotiation is always possible, and furthermore it is desirable. Conversely, Al-Qaeda-type transnational terrorism seeks to attack the "system" in general: it has no concrete objectives and believes more in propaganda through action. Here, nothing is negotiable, because there are two different arenas.

The refusal to distinguish between movements which are primarily political and others which are purely terrorist, makes action impossible. There is not the military capability to attack on all fronts: it is not possible simultaneously to wage war on Al-Qaeda, the Taliban, Hezbollah, Hamas, Syria and Iran (and the Muslim Brotherhood, veiled women, inner-city imams etc.). This refusal also makes it impossible to classify the conflicts according to the threat they represent and above all to negotiate with the movements or states with which a conflict could effectively be resolved. Or else undercover negotiations involving the secret services take place, devoid of any principles and even involving corruption and dirty tricks, such as during Irangate (when those close to President Reagan defied the embargo and sold arms to Iran to finance the anti-Sandinista *contras* in Nicaragua), or certain negotiations to secure the release of hostages. The purity of the discourse is belied by an unprincipled practice which discredits the idea of fair combat. If terrorism is defined so broadly, then the idea that there can be no compromise with the terrorists is no more than a virtuous con. In 1956, Nasser was called the "new Hitler" by the French and British press, only for praise to be heaped on his successor, Sadat, twenty years later, promoter of peace with Israel. In the 1970s, Arafat was seen as a terrorist, but in 2007, his successor, Mahmoud Abbas was supported against Hamas. And sooner or later, we will have to resign ourselves to negotiating with Hamas and Hezbollah to stop Al-Qaeda infiltrating Lebanon and Palestine.

Concretely, in the current Middle East climate, if independence is to be restored to Lebanon and the Hezbollah-Damascus-Tehran and Hezbollah-Hamas axes broken, negotiating with some of the actors is going to be unavoidable. What will count is not their position on the "terrorism" ladder, but their willingness to be part of the most acceptable political solution for all concerned, starting with the most stable. That is why, when in 2006 the Europeans (and especially President Chirac) shunned a Syrian regime accused (rightly) of assassinating the former Lebanese Prime Minister Rafiq Hariri, the Israelis negotiated in secret with Bashar al Asad's Syria.[13]

Moral intransigence leads to impotence if based on a non-political definition of evil.

Islamism and neo-fundamentalism

In the public mind, today the term Islamism means all forms of Islamic radicalism. It is not possible to fight shifting meanings, but it is useful to clarify the way words are used. Let us

---

13 See *Haaretz*, 17 January 2007

return to the concept. Islamism in the strict sense of the word is, in my view, the political ideologisation of Islam, on the model of the great political ideologies of the 20th century (Marxism and fascism but not Nazism), which has nothing to do with terrorism.

The failure of political Islam is not that of the activists, but of the ideology underpinning the establishment of an Islamic state capable of instigating effective and legitimate political institutions and social justice, and guaranteeing economic development (according to this model, *sharia* is subservient to the institutions). It does not work, as all the aftermaths of victory show (Iran, Afghanistan), and there are complex reasons for this: political, national and even ethnic or tribal loyalties have a more powerful hold than ideology; societies become secular when faced with the impasse of religious ideology; corruption makes the myth of the virtuous leader meaningless, etc. That leaves the Islamists two options: the transition to a Muslim-style Christian democracy (based on a model that is more Bavarian than Neapolitan)—that is the Turkish model with the AK party and Prime Minister Erdogan; or the transition to a neofundamentalism interested in neither state nor nation, but which seeks to transform the individual according to a rigid model of religion defined as the strict application of *sharia*.

57

This neofundamentalism, initially more anti-Communist than anti-Western, became radicalised in the wake of the Islamist movements' failure to establish credible Islamic states, for it revived the Islamists' militant anti-Western tradition that was running out of steam. It embraces the Afghan Taliban and Al-Qaeda, Saudi Wahhabism (the school of Sunni Islam based on the teachings of the late 18th-century scholar Abdul Wahhab, adopted by the al-Saud dynasty), Salafism of every hue, which wants to revert solely to the Qur'an and the Tradition of the Prophet, and the Tabligh movement, founded in 1926 to bring Muslims back to the "true" Islam, etc. This neofundamentalism, deterritorialised and decultured by definition, is perfectly adapted to globalisation, which explains its success. It is split into two wings. The first, conservative, apolitical, but culturally separatist, subscribes to the concept of multiculturalism. The second, jihadist, takes up the legacy of the anti-imperialist violence of the European far left, but can just as well borrow from the anti-Semitic, anti-modernist far right. Jihadist radicalisation affects the "deterritorialised", i.e. those whose actions do not fit into a national and territorial project. That is the Al-Qaeda model.

Of course, the boundaries between all these tendencies are not impermeable, and the paths taken by individuals can lead them in one direction (towards democracy: Erdogan) or the other (towards terrorism: Ayman al Zawahiri). But there will be no democratisation of the Muslim world without the integration of the Islamists who have chosen the first avenue, that of political integration and democracy. Any attempt to put words into their mouths would be to ignore the fact that a politician is made up not so much of absolute convictions but of the internalised rules of the political game. The choice is indeed between Erdogan and the Taliban.

For the supporters of a fully secular democracy, the problem is that for the time being there is no democratic alternative to the moderate Islamists. If in the Maghreb there is a strong tension between secular and Islamist, the former tend rather to ally themselves with strong regimes or to go into exile. Conversely, in the Middle East, this tension has almost disappeared: the conflict between Hamas and Fatah is not ideological; it does not oppose two different models of Palestinian society. The secular nationalists are on the same side as the Islamists; in other words, the rift is not over *sharia*. The conflicts are not shaped by ideology, be it in Lebanon, where General Aoun's Christians are allied to Hezbollah, Palestine, where other Christians are close to the Sunnis, Turkey, where it is the nationalist far right that embodies radical anti-Western violence, or Iraq, where the divisions are between Shia and Sunnis or Kurds and Arabs. None of these are clashes between secular and Islamist; in fact not one conflict in the Middle East can be described as a conflict between secular and Islamist. The tolerance towards Islamic movements shown by nationalist intellectuals in Pakistan and Egypt, in the name of authenticity and resistance to Western influence, is striking: the Pakistani intelligentsia were mostly opposed to the American intervention against the Taliban; in Egypt, few intellectuals protested against the trial of the "homosexuals" in 2005, however they did express their bewilderment over the French law banning the wearing of the headscarf at school. In defining prohibitions as the defence of social and cultural values and no longer as a purely religious norm, the fundamentalists and authoritarian regimes mobilise much broader public support than just among the grassroots Islamists. In short, there are countless examples, but nowhere in the Middle East is there a war with the Islamists on one side and the secular democrats on the other, whereas media debates in Europe give the impression that that is the main division.

The structural fragility of secular dictatorships stems from the weak position of the supporters of both *realpolitik* and authoritarian secularism. These exacerbate the tensions by excluding any possibility of a third way between them and Islamism. In the little game of "me or Islamism", the Islamists soon appear to be the only credible opposition in the eyes of the population. These regimes are no longer a bulwark against an Islamisation which is increasingly taking on the colours of democracy (Tunisia, Saudi Arabia, Jordan, Egypt). Besides, they have no hesitation in playing the Islamisation card themselves by making gestures to the conservative mullahs, even if they are opposed to the external signs of this Islam (e.g. the banning of the veil in Tunisia). They are an obstacle to economic development due to the corruption of the ruling elites who very often hinder the emergence of a class of national entrepreneurs and foreign investment. And such regimes can only find legitimacy by playing on a nationalism that is often anti-Western (in Syria, or even Algeria where France is concerned), even if their rulers claim to be on the best terms with their European counterparts, the French in particular (Algeria, Egypt). The Maghreb is again becoming fertile ground for all forms of Islamic protest and Tunisia is certainly one of the weakest links.

So what is the impact of the Islamist movements? In a paroxystic situation, in other words when free elections are suddenly held after years of turmoil and corruption, their count can reach or exceed 50%, as in Algeria in 1990-1991, or in Palestine in 2006, except when the voting follows community allegiances rather than an ideology, as in Iraq in 2006, as would probably be the case in Morocco and in Egypt if sudden elections were to be held. But when the political scene is stable, Islamists tend to garner around 20% (the maximum count of the Refah Party in Turkey, and of Ahmadinejad in Iran in the first round of the presidential elections in June 2005). To do better, Islamists either have to enter into a coalition or seek votes outside their traditional support base. To do that, they need a broader programme than *sharia* and the Islamic state: that is why the Turkish AK broke with the Refah's legacy and was able to win the 2002 elections with 34.3% of the vote. It is clear that the Palestinians who voted for Hamas in 2006 did not do so because they wanted the destruction of Israel or *sharia*, but because they wanted good governance, like the Iranians who supported Ahmadinejad in the second round of the Iranian presidential elections in 2005. This issue of good governance and the fight against corruption, coupled with that of the defence of the nation and resistance to American influence, will remain critical for a long time to come.

Only the gradual opening up of a political arena with the restoration of freedom of expression and the establishment of a proper judicial system can prompt the centrist Islamists to accept democracy and the rule of law.

Sharia and totalitarianism

Sharia is often spoken of as the expression of an Islamic totalitarianism. Here the confusion is total. *Sharia* can be criticised for being anachronistic and misogynistic, but *sharia* remains in all cases a law, with its norms and its interpreters. It is not in itself arbitrary, and it defines a legal space, in particular in the private sphere (the notion of *haram*). It is a legal system that claims to be independent from positive law, i.e. state law, whatever the politics of that state (even an Islamic state). In the eyes of the neofundamentalists, the state can only declare that *sharia* is the law of the land and must then stop legislating, except on secondary matters. The wholesale application of *sharia* means the end of the all-powerful state; it is therefore incompatible with totalitarianism in the strict sense of the word. Totalitarianism can only be characteristic of a state that is able to maintain a hold over people's minds through a propaganda and control machine (even if we now know the extent to which the Soviet and Nazi systems' bureaucratic plumbing was plagued by leaks). That is why there has never been any society living totally under *sharia*, because no government is prepared to commit suicide. The *sharia* society is a myth, be it nightmare or utopia. *Sharia* is destined to be the permanent aporia of any state claiming to be Islamic. Such states have attempted to resolve the question in three different ways:

— by confining *sharia* to the personal sphere, family law and anything to do with morality, with everything else falling within the province of positive law (till today, this is the most frequent compromise);

— by completely separating *sharia* from the rules governing accession to power, while declaring it state law. That is the Saudi preference, which is of course schizophrenic as it makes the power of the dynasty seem purely contingent and not based in law. It is also the formula of the Taliban in Afghanistan;

— by asserting that political principles, in the Islamic state too, supersede those of *sharia*: this is the choice made by the imam Khomeini in Iran on several occasions (the banning of pilgrimages in 1987, even though they are a religious obligation, the authorisation of nocturnal house searches, which could bring a man into contact with an unveiled woman, or worse...).

The impossibility of founding a society on the exclusive basis of *sharia* is of course a source of tension which enables increasingly radical groups to promise that *sharia* will at last be implemented. But it also explains why things inevitably return to the issue of the family, in other words, of women, since in the last analysis, in a modern society it is the only place where *sharia* has any real autonomy. In fact, the position of women and apostasy are the two (and the only) touchstones on the question of Islam's compatibility with "Western values".

Cultural Islam and the myth of Eurabia

A whole series of recently published books explore the theme of the Islamisation of Europe.[14] They offer a distinctly geostrategic vision: that of a tectonic shift in which the Middle East will gain ground in Europe through demographic expansion. This would only make sense if every person of Muslim origin were considered to be a carrier of some sort of genetic atavism, an internalised Muslim culture whose values are intrinsically opposed to those of the West.

This fixed, essentialist vision, bordering on the kind of unbridled racism that is found in Oriana Fallaci's book, *The Rage and the Pride*, obviously ignores the profound effects of mobility and globalisation in transforming Islam and Muslims. This notion of a monolithic Islamic culture does not take account of the changes, recompositions,

---

14 For instance Bat Yeor's *Eurabia*, not to mention Bernard Lewis's numerous writings and conference speeches.

syncretisms and deculturation specific to globalisation that are occurring, even if they do create tensions and violence. The tensions stirring up Islam are rather the corollary of an often turbulent integration. Modern Salafism is both the consequence and an agent of this deculturation and in no way expresses the reaction of a traditional society refusing modernisation.

The idea that Europe supposedly embodies liberalism by definition, while Islam represents conservatism, muddies the debate on today's Western values, which is not a clash between the Orient and the West, but, for example, between "pro-choice" and "pro-life" supporters, those who accept gay marriage and those who don't, advocates of total human freedom as opposed to those who cling to a natural or divine order, especially in bioethics or in the sphere of freedom of expression. Coalitions, whose geometry is often variable, form to defend certain values, bringing together "Western" Catholics, Evangelists, Jews, and Muslims. One such example is the interreligious declaration of Lyons against gay marriage, issued in February 2007 by the Archbishop of Lyons, Philippe Barbarin, and signed by Rabbi Wertenschlag, Kamel Kebtane, the rector of the mosque and local Evangelist leaders. The strange pairing created by France's Fillon government in 2007 between the Catholic fundamentalist Christine Boutin and Fadela Amara, an "eradicator" of Muslim origin, also shows that alliances have little to do with slogans.

Essentialist and paranoid hysteria does not lead to any kind of concrete strategy. What is more, it naturally goes hand in hand with a profound pessimism as to the future of humanity (here identified with the West), which perfectly echoes that of the radical jihadists themselves. For if one accepts its assumptions (demography spreads Islam), then it is too late: all that remains is to identify the "traitors" who let the wolf into the sheep pen.[15]

What is the geostrategic impact of the establishment of Islam in Europe? Allegedly everything that would create a continuum between the Middle East and Europe for the benefit of the former: importation of the Israeli-Palestinian conflict, an Islamic fifth column, the role of national diasporas in the event of tensions or conflicts, etc. However re-Islamisation does not reinforce organic links with movements and countries in the Middle East, rather it promotes

---

15 The traitors are always the liberal left, the politically correct, the multiculturalists, the Third-Worldists. Note a fairly interesting variation: Dinesh D'Souza's book, which suggests that the American intellectual left is a much more dangerous enemy than Al-Qaeda. See Dinesh D'Souza, *The Enemy at Home: The Cultural Left and Its Responsibility for 9/11*, Doubleday, 2006.

a deterritorialised religious identity which, on the contrary, eludes the control of the Muslim states. Recent events in France showed that the "Intifada of the suburbs" was a myth: during the riots of 2005 no Palestinian flags were unfurled in the suburbs, no Qur'ans either. The very rare pro-Palestinian demonstrations held in Paris attract barely 15,000 people, and they include a good number of greying lefties, whereas there are hundreds of thousands of people, even millions, who could call themselves Muslim in the capital and the suburbs. It is not the Middle East that galvanises the Muslim population in France, but rather those who are active around this Muslim population.

We must stop speaking of a diaspora. Second and third-generation immigrants lose their language and culture of origin. What was unexpected was that the trend would not always be assimilation, but possibly the building of a "faith community", founded on a virtual *ummah* (transnational community of believers), a radicalisation which would not necessarily reactivate the diaspora's connections. Today's young radicals generally have no organic links with the "jihad" they are joining. No French youths of Algerian origin joined the underground GIA in Algeria; they preferred Bosnia, Chechnya or Afghanistan. In Britain, those who flare up in outrage at the government's policy towards the Arab world are generally Pakistanis or converts. There are no Palestinians or Afghans among the perpetrators of attacks in the West committed in protest against Western involvement in Palestine, Afghanistan or Iraq. The over-representation of Pakistanis in the British jihadist movements is primarily because British Muslims chiefly originate from the Indian sub-continent, but above all because Pakistan defines itself outside the model of the territorialised nation-state: it is an ideological state which has succeeded in rallying its citizens around the issues of transnationality.

Most Muslims in Europe aspire to integration. There are a number of explanations for the British exception:[16] alliance with the political far left, the importance of the Pakistani paradigm, the influence of faith schools in the educational system, the policy of multiculturalism which has led to a "separate" identity... It is therefore linked more to specific British (and Pakistani) circumstances than to that of Islam.

Oddly, the European governments, who call for an Islam of Europe (and not in Europe), are forever re-forging links between their Muslims and the Middle East, thus reinforc-

---

16 See the survey *Muslims in Europe: Economic Worries Top Concerns About Religious and Cultural Identity*, Pew Global Attitudes Project, 2006.

ing their status as outsiders. The French government, after having created the Conseil Français du Culte Musulman (CFCM, French Muslim Council) as the organ of French Islam, allied itself with Moroccan diplomatic circles to influence the 2005 elections to the CFCM. French ministers went to Cairo to seek a *fatwa* endorsing the law banning the headscarf in 2004. In 2005, the same government sent the CFCM to Iraq to negotiate the release of French hostages. The Danish government mobilised its diplomats (unsuccessfully) to handle the Danish cartoon crisis, without consulting its Muslim community. Until the end of the 1990s, it was compulsory in the Netherlands for second-generation schoolchildren to be taught their languages of origin. The Spanish government adopted the concept of "dialogue of civilisations" without seeing that it was based on the same assumptions as that of the clash (i.e. that all cultures are based on a religion and all religions are expressed in a culture). In short, the European governments worry about the consequences of the presence of a diaspora reputedly foreign to Western values, without being very clear themselves as to the meaning and practice of citizenship. The only coherent policy would be to promote full citizenship and social integration instead of "multiculturalism", which maintains Muslims as perpetual aliens.

All this is quite far removed from the initial preoccupations of the American neoconservatives who at least believed in the universality of values. The discussion today is focused on the compatibility of Islam with—according to preference—democracy, Western values, human rights (and women's rights), secularism, etc., but the jump from these questions to that of Muslims' compatibility with Europe is often hastily made. The notion of Eurabia reconnects the Muslims of Europe to outside conflicts which barely affect them.

The geostrategy in vogue does not recognise geographical or cultural constraints; it is a self-fulfilling prophecy for it transforms an imagined situation into a policy and therefore gives substance to this new essentialist dogma, which can be heard everywhere, from the pub to the ministerial office and now even among people who like to call themselves philosophers.

Indisputably, 9/11 changed our world, but not in that it signalled the emergence of a new force or a new power. This is not the Sarajevo assassination of 1914, nor the storming of the Winter Palace by the Bolsheviks, nor the burning of the Reichstag in 1933, for in all these cases state powers fought each other to capture territories. The fascist, Nazi and Communist ideologies served to mobilise the populations for war, they were instrumentalised by the state apparatus, foreign sympathisers served as a fifth column or seized on these ideologies to develop their own nationalism. Meanwhile the true internationalists were never able to impose their ideals and died as martyrs, traitors or pawns. And when liberation movements took hold of ideologies such as Marxism, and later Islamism, they still operated from a nationalist, state and territorial perspective.

2

THE MIDDLE EAST: FRAGMENTATION OF CONFLICTS AND NEW FAULT LINES

The vision of a Muslim world at war with the West is a fantasy. This "Muslim world" does not exist. Most of the conflicts affecting the Middle East involve Muslims against Muslims. The current regimes mostly describe themselves as allies of the West. Furthermore, this explains why President Ahmadinejad's Iran is seeking allies among the populists of Latin America rather than among its neighbours.

Islamisation only becomes a strategic factor when it converges with another current, in general nationalist (as with Hamas or Iran), ethnic or tribal (all three of these categories apply to the Taliban). The complexity of this interplay of alliances contrasts with the demagogic simplicity of the slogan "global war on terror". In Iraq, the Americans are giving arms-length support to a government that is close to their bitterest enemy, Iran. Al-Qaeda has taken refuge in a country that is supposedly an ally of the West, Pakistan, which almost openly supports the Taliban in its war against the new Afghan regime established by the international community. In Lebanon, the Shia Hezbollah has joined forces with General Aoun's Christians in an alliance that is a greater threat to the Sunni Muslims than to the Maronite Christians. The Syrian regime, which backs Hezbollah, massacred and imprisoned the Muslim Brotherhood. Saudi Arabia, a long-standing ally of the United States and whose royal family has continually forged close links with the Republican establishment, is the source of the most anti-Western forms of Islam, while discreetly drawing closer to Israel in the face of their new common enemy, an Iran with a nuclear capability. Clearly, there is a lot of hypocrisy and secrecy in all this: the day the United States bombs Iran, all the Arab capitals will protest, but more than one will be quietly jubilant.

THE THREE TRAUMAS OF THE ARAB MIDDLE EAST

Three fault lines, or traumas, mark the contemporary history of the Arab Middle East, and not one of them has anything to do with Islam as such. Rather they raise the problem of "Arabness", or the translation of an Arab identity into political terms. The first, in 1918, was the collapse of the project to build a great Arab kingdom out of the ruins of the Ottoman Empire, as promised by the British. The second is the establishment of the state of Israel and the failure of the four wars (1948, 1956, 1967, 1973) to destroy, reduce or counter it. The third is the destruction of the balance between Shi'ism and Sunnism, which occurred in two stages: the Islamic revolution in Iran, whose expansion was first of all blocked by the Iraq of Saddam Hussein, then by Iraq's swing towards Shi'ism following the American intervention of 2003. This sudden change coincides with Hezbollah taking the lead in the anti-Israel refusal front in the aftermath of the brief war of July 2006.

The Arabs had risen up alongside the Allies during World War I to crush the Ottoman Empire, even though it claimed to be in favour of the Caliphate and had entered the war on the side of Germany in 1914 proclaiming jihad against the English and the French. The Allies were already colonial powers in the African part of this empire (from Algeria to Egypt). Nevertheless, the Arabs overwhelmingly chose to support the Allies against the great Muslim power of the day, in the name of Arab nationalism. It is significant that, from this time, Arab nationalism was far more powerful a force than pan-Islamism and the call to jihad. This uprising was very much in keeping with 19th-century European nationalisms based on the correspondence between a territory and an ethnic and linguistic group (which also applies to Zionism). Similarly it mirrored the shift among the Ottomans themselves, with the Young Turks before 1914, then Ataturk after 1918, also adopting an ethnic and linguistic vision of the nation, at the expense of the imperial ideology defended by the sultan and the multi-ethnic character of the Empire. But the Allies played a double game. On the one hand, the British promised a great Arab kingdom, ruled by the Hashemite dynasty, at the time in charge of the Holy Places (this is the epic of Lawrence of Arabia); on the other, through the Sykes-Picot Agreement (1916), France and Britain divided between them the Arab lands abandoned by the Ottoman armies.

The first trauma for the Arab world between Suez and Iran was therefore this unforeseen re-colonisation and the carving up of the area into new states. The Allies grouped the Ottoman provinces (*vilayet*) in combinations that suited their strategic interests at the time. The idea of an independent Armenia and Kurdistan was jettisoned, Mosul was annexed to Iraq and thus the division of the Middle East into only three ethnic groups—Turks, Arabs and Persians—

while waiting for the Jewish homeland to be transformed into a state, was endorsed. Lebanon, Transjordan and Iraq were literally fabricated, and Syria was reduced in size. The British meanwhile accepted the establishment of a "Jewish homeland" in Palestine enshrined in the Balfour declaration (1917). And lastly, the victory of the Al Sauds over the Hashemites (the British had in fact encouraged both rival families vying for the custodianship of the Holy Places of Islam) separated off Arabia, which became "Saudi", from the two kingdoms (Transjordan and Iraq) controlled by the Hashemites. The dream of a great Arab kingdom stretching from the Mediterranean to Mesopotamia was dead. Of course, it is likely that even if the Allies had effectively handed over this area to King Faisal, it would have ended up being split, but along different lines. The fact remains that today the blame for this division is laid at the feet of the West.

The second trauma is the creation of the State of Israel in 1948, at the precise moment when the Arab states had just gained full independence and were flaunting projects for Arab unity to erase the failure of 1918. In the Middle East, Israel was seen as a Western bridgehead, an extension of the great division effected between 1918 and 1922. The presence of Israel was to revive a pan-Arab nationalism, but in a negative way, as it was defined by being what it was against rather than for. All the attempts to give a political and territorial expression to this pan-Arabism failed miserably, the most noteworthy being the United Arab Republic, which brought together Egypt and Syria from 1958 to 1961. The Ba'ath party, founded in 1947 to embody this pan-Arabism (a party which is actually secular and in which Arab Christians played a prominent role), defines each Arab country as a "region", and reserves the title of "nation" for all the Arab countries. Although it took power in Syria and Iraq the same year (1963), instead of merging, the two countries immediately fell out. This led to a split in the party, and above all confusion in both countries, between the party and the ruling group.

Secular Arabism no longer had a transnational instrument (unlike Islamic pan-Arabism, personified by the Muslim Brotherhood). The inability to defeat Israel, or to integrate the Palestinian refugees, shattered political pan-Arabism. Resignation over Israel's existence gradually set in—the most spectacular sign of this being the recognition of the Jewish state by Egypt under President Sadat (Israel-Egypt Peace Treaty of 1979). The failure of the Oslo process came just at the point when many Israelis felt convinced that peace with the Arabs was impossible, and it was then that signs of the Arab states' resignation became most evident: an end to the arms race to achieve an unattainable strategic equality, distance with regard to the Palestinians—notably since Hamas's victory—, barely concealed criticism of Hezbollah and growing concern over the rise of a common enemy, Iran. Israel is no longer confronted by Arab states, but by movements, such as Hamas and Hezbollah. And so today there is a historic opportunity to make peace, but it will probably be lost.

The third trauma is unfolding before our eyes: the Sunni Arabs' political supremacy in the Middle East in the area to the east of Suez is being eroded because whatever the outcome, Iraq will no longer be a Sunni Arab state. If it remains an Arab state, it will be Shia; if there is partition or anarchy, there will no longer be a state; and if Iran establishes a protectorate (the least likely scenario), Iraq will no longer be Arab.

The only stable boundary of the Ottoman Empire was the border with Iran, running from the southern Caucasus to the Persian Gulf and determined by the Treaty of Zuhab (or the Peace of Qasr-e Shirin) in 1639. Having withstood the upheavals of the demise of the Ottoman Empire and the intervention of the Western powers, it remained inviolable until the American military intervention in Iraq in 2003.

Today it constitutes the border between Turkey and Iraq on the one hand, and Iran on the other. The only disputed point was the Shatt el Arab, the river that is the continuation of the Tigris and the Euphrates in the Persian Gulf: was the frontier (of roughly 100 km.) on the Iranian shore or down the middle of the river? This was the cause of tensions in the 1970s, then of the 1980 Iran-Iraq war, and it was agreed that the frontier ran down the middle. This border is neither ethnic nor religious; there are Arabs, Kurds and Turks as well as Sunnis and Shia on both sides. But it has a more important significance: politically, it divides the Sunni Arab world from the Iranian Shia world. It makes Shi'ism an Iranian phenomenon and ignores the specificity of Arab branches of Shi'ism. The Shia Arab populations to the west of this border were therefore placed under the political authority of the Sunnis, firstly Ottoman, then, after 1918, Arab. This frontier is therefore one of the few stable strategic elements in the region. But it has just disappeared, for even if Iraq remains a nation-state, the true boundary now divides Shia and Sunnis inside Iraq as a result of a series of attacks, each leading to populations being displaced towards areas that are demographically homogeneous (this is also true of Kurdistan).

Iran's increased influence and the quasi-independence of Iraqi Kurdistan to the east, coupled with Israeli dominance over the Palestinians who are on the brink of civil war and the rise of the Shia Hezbollah in Lebanon to the west, have resulted in the shrinking of the Sunni Arab area.

NATIONALISM, CLANNISM AND SUPRANATIONALISM: A CRISIS OF THE POLITICAL IMAGINATION

A major problem in the Middle East is that of political legitimacy. Local nationalisms generally develop around states, not regimes, but the political ideologies on the market are supra-nationalist while the political "grammar" (the game of individual alliances and loyalties) is inter-state (all that is contained in the term *asabiyya or* "solidarity group": clannism, tribalism, sectarianism).[1] Unlike in Turkey or Iran, national patriotisms are not easily accepted and hide behind supra-national ideological discourses. But these supranational ideologies (pan-Arabism, pan-Islamism, "pan-Shi'ism") simultaneously overlap and vie with each other. And so there is a gap between an imaginary political utopia which is virtual and always a failure, and concrete political practice (a mix of nationalism and *asabiyya*) which

---

1   See Faleh Jabar and Hosham Dawod (eds), *Tribes and Power: Nationalism and Ethnicity in the Middle East*, Saqi, 2003.

finds it hard to come to terms with itself. And yet nationalisms remain the key to conflicts, but are undermined by internal divisions (ethnic and faith rivalries in Iraq, Lebanon and Afghanistan; tensions between Shia and Sunnis; transformations of the tribal system) which can be linked to ideologies and transnational networks. This discrepancy leaves the way open to all sorts of conspiracy theories and all kinds of frustration.

Inescapable nationalism

Each local conflict has its own history and follows its own course, the most striking examples being the rivalry between Iran and Iraq, which echoes the border battle between the Persian and Ottoman empires, or Pakistan in its endless quest for legitimacy and territory, the Palestinian and Israeli peoples' difficulty in making the transition from an existential to a territorial conflict, Syria's refusal to accept Lebanon's independence, Pakistan's instrumentalisation of Afghanistan and Kashmir in its competition with India, or the conflict between Ethiopia and Somalia. Today, as in the past, Hamas and jihad's quarrel with Fatah is not religious, but centres on its alleged betrayal of the interests of the Palestinian people. In Lebanon, Hezbollah has always presented its struggle in the south of the country as a struggle to liberate the national homeland. The Algerian FIS claimed to be part of the "true" FLN, which had fought the French. The Muslim Brotherhood has always been divided into national chapters, a far cry from the fantasy of the "Islamist International". And when, in September 1980, Iraq invaded Iran, not a single Arab Islamist militant sided with the Islamic revolution. A decade later, during the 1991 Gulf War, the national branches of the Muslim Brotherhood took sides according to the interests of their respective countries: the Jordanians were against calling in Western troops while the Kuwaitis were for it.

The political framework is first of all national. Everywhere, immigration and nationality legislation is very restrictive, the status of refugees precarious, even when they are Arabs and Muslims. Everywhere, state thinking and popular demagogy tend to exclude the "other", even if they are Muslim (Palestinians in Lebanon, Afghans in Iran, the bitter experience of Malians in Libya). In Iran, a Shia Afghan Farsi speaker who wants to marry an Iranian woman has to go through the same rigorous process as a non-Muslim European (who must, in theory, convert). In the Gulf Emirates, states and public opinion alike are outraged at the high number of marriages to "foreign" women (the bride price for local women having shot up exponentially). Only

Jordan has integrated the Palestinian refugees of 1948. The same pro-Palestine crowds that demonstrate in Cairo would be opposed to granting Egyptian nationality to the mass of Palestinian refugees. The American intervention in Iraq has seen a repeat of this pattern: people claim solidarity with the Iraqis against the Americans, but the two million Iraqi refugees who settle in other Arab countries encounter the hostility of the local population.

Nationalist conflicts can of course be expressed in terms of changing ideological thinking across the entire Greater Middle East. Zionism and the Palestinian movement have both been positioned from the outset as secular nationalisms and not religious movements. The first war between Ethiopia and Somalia over the Ogaden in 1976 pitted two socialist regimes and allies of the USSR against each other; the Ethiopian intervention in Somalia in December 2006 to rid it of the Union of Islamic Courts appears to be a battle against Islamism, but the issues are just as equally nationalist. Islamisation of the resistance in Kashmir was encouraged by Pakistan from the 1980s, precisely to prevent Kashmiri nationalism from breaking away from Pakistan or reaching a compromise with India, to the detriment of Pakistan. Finally, it is the Islamic Republic of Iran, established in 1979, which interpreted the conflict between

Iran and Iraq in religious terms. It had been latent in the Shah's era, but was then thought of as a confrontation between Persians and Arabs. During the war between Iraq and Iran, Ayatollah Khomeini coined the slogan "the road to Jerusalem goes through Karbala", which meant: before we can fight Israel, first of all we have to get rid of Saddam Hussein. It is precisely for this reason that Sunni Arab Islamist movements (the Muslim Brotherhood, for example) have refused to support Islamic Iran against the conservative Arab regimes, even though the latter repress them.

Moreover, states have instrumentalised ideologies (Nasser's Egypt, Ba'athist Syria and Iraq did so with pan-Arabism, as did Iran, Saudi Arabia and Pakistan with different forms of pan-Islamism). But the opposite is not true: the Muslim Brotherhood did not succeed in harnessing Arab nationalism.[2] Since 2003, Salafism made a similar attempt to exploit Arab nationalism in the wake of the American

2   An interesting example of an attempted synthesis between pan-Islamism and Arab nationalism is the Hizb ut-Tahrir (HT), formed in Jordan in 1953 by Sheikh Nabhani, a Palestinian Muslim Brother, disillusioned by what he saw as the half-hearted attitude of the Egyptian Brotherhood towards the Palestinians. Called "the Liberation Party", campaigning for an Islamic Caliphate, in thirty years HT became a supra-national, globalised movement based in London and advocating a global, deterritorialised Caliphate. On the other hand, in Jordan a branch of the party still survives as a regional movement.

military intervention in Iraq, when thousands of Arab volunteers tried to make their way to Falluja. At the same time, in the complex game between the Pakistani regime and the radical movements based on its territory, one may wonder who is using whom: is the national state using the radicals in its regional policy, or is it the radicals who are wary of destroying a state that is officially an ally of the United States and consequently shelters them from any American threat? We must return then to the dialectic of the relations between nationalism and supranationalism.

This nationalist affirmation is very ambiguous, as it is a cross between a sense of local allegiance—Syrian, Iraqi, Lebanese, Egyptian, and even Saudi[3]—and a feeling of pan-Arab supranational identity. Often a legacy of colonisation, the state framework is simultaneously demanded by the region's populations but also rejected. The conflicts are structural insofar as they are inherent in the very creation of the countries concerned. They rarely go back a long way (except for the border between Iran and its Sunni neighbours, established in the 17th century), dating from two postwar periods: the 1920s and the late 1940s, with

---

3   While Al-Qaeda's members in Saudi Arabia refuse to call the country by that name, the secular opponents keep the adjective "Saudi", even though they object to the dynasty; see the *Saudi Institute* established in Washington under the directorship of Ali Al Ahmed.

independence and the withdrawal of the colonial powers. In many respects, the nationalist renaissance is experienced in a schizophrenic manner, all the more so since the state, here as elsewhere, is damaged by the economic, cultural and human effects of globalisation. In this context, identity tends to take refuge in a cultural imagination, where Islam is very effective, as long as it is grafted onto the pan-Arab ideal. We are therefore witnessing the Islamisation of Arabism. The civilisational divide expressed by the Huntingtonian thesis of the clash of civilisations is more popular in the Middle East, not because it expresses a traditional cultural identity, but on the contrary a recasting of pan-Arabism into a Muslim religious identity. Hence the success of Salafism. The lack of a real political perspective to fulfil the pan-Arab as well as pan-Islamic dream has led to a reversion to conservative cultural and social values, which creates fertile ground for Salafism.

Ethnic groups, faith communities and tribes

The problem is complicated by the fact that many of these states are divided along community lines which can be religious (Lebanon, Iraq, Syria, Kuwait, Saudi Arabia, Bahrain), ethnic (Pakistan, Afghanistan, Iraq), or even simply tribal (Somalia, Yemen). Now these groups also tend to become international or at least link up with international networks. "Tribalism" in the broader sense is often perceived as a closed, traditional system where allegiances are determined solely by belonging to the group, and certainly it is true that tribalism plays a role in solidarity networks and local conflicts. But we must not overlook rivalries between Shia tribes in Iraq, leading Maronite families in Lebanon or Alawite clans in Syria, or instances where horizontal solidarity may ensure cooperation and protection between members of the same group belonging to rival political camps.

But tribes are open to the world. The tribal system is not disappearing; it is adapting to globalisation and to supranational ideologies. A recurrent phenomenon is the Islamisation of tribal groups, e.g. Afghan and Pakistani Pushtuns, Somali clans, Yemeni tribes. Here again, the rise of Islamism can be explained by transformations of traditional societies. In Yemen, as in Afghanistan and Pakistan, and probably also in Saudi Arabia, the clergy, mullahs and sheikhs are substitutes for traditional tribal leaders, but this competition does not translate into armed struggle. At the same time, demanding *sharia* is a way of continuing to oppose the central state, but this time not in a local, reactive way, in the name of particularisms and traditional customs, but on the contrary, by presenting itself as being directly linked to the *ummah* and by pushing the central state into particularism. The tribe continues to exist by projecting itself onto the world, which often goes hand in hand with economic globalisation (involvement in drug trafficking, smuggling, the migration of workers). One and a half million Pushtuns from the tribal regions, both Pakistani and Afghan, live in Karachi; it is they who run road transport in the city and elsewhere. In Yemen, the northern tribes have migrated in large numbers to the Gulf and Saudi Arabia—those from the Hadramaut district have a very ancient tradition of emigration to Britain and Indonesia. And so it would be a mistake to present this Islamisation purely as a new means of expressing irredentism: here, on the contrary, tribalism surpasses itself.

Conversely, tribal groups where Islam does not play a major role can develop a nationalist identity, as the Kurds have done. The Pakistani Baluchi tribes are also building an identity that is antagonistic to the Pushtuns, whose expansion threatens the ethnic identity of Baluchistan. The secular and secularised Baluchis have retained the traditional tribal hierarchy and wage their struggle under the leadership of the Sardars, who, since the 1970s, have been cultivating "left-wing" alliances (USSR, the Communist regime in Kabul). So there is a frequent discrepancy between such "progressive" references and the archaism of the tribal system, and it is often Islamist or neofundamentalist-type movements that are best suited to globalisation. This explains why the current conflict between the Baluchis and the Pakistani state is not mentioned in the international media, as it does not correspond to the fashionable stereotype.

This same globalisation process also prompts faith groups to define themselves in relation to a global identity. That is the whole ambiguity of Hezbollah, born as the party of the south Lebanese Shia—a population that traditionally has been marginalised in Lebanon—which then declares itself a Lebanese political party and goes on to link up to the international Shia revolution.

But this question concerns essentially the Middle East to the east of Suez. In the North African area of the Greater Middle East (the Maghreb, Libya, Egypt), it is less of a consideration. This area is relatively stable from the point of view of the definition of nation states and ethnic balances. There is indeed a border dispute between Morocco and Algeria, which came to a head over the question of the Western Sahara, annexed *de facto* by Morocco after the departure of the Spanish, but it remains marginal. The tensions over the status of the Berbers in Morocco, and above all the Kabyles in Algeria, hardly undermine the nation state.

Egypt is ethnically homogeneous and the friction between Muslims and Copts does not affect the Copts' patriotism, or even Egyptian and Arab nationalism which is promoted by Pope Shenouda of the Coptic Orthodox Church. As for Libya, Gaddafi's versatility and eccentricities have led to the failure of all his grand plans to reshape the strategic landscape by sometimes playing the pan-Arab and sometimes the pan-African card.

Tribalism and clannism certainly exist in all the Maghreb states; we know that the conflicts in southern Egypt, even when they take the form of political or faith disputes, have a lot to do with local vendettas (*tar*). But this local tribalism has nothing to do with the clan struggles that shake the ruling powers, remaining at the infra-political level, which is much less the case in the Middle East proper.

FROM PAN-ARABISM TO PAN-ISLAMISM

The secular pan-Arabism of Nasser and the Ba'ath therefore failed; it was instrumentalised by various regimes but was not able to supersede national identities. The political vision of pan-Arabism however is alive and well: it relies on a very strong emotive power but no longer has any political underpinning. Pan-Islamism in its various forms becomes a substitute both for the expansion of pan-Arabism (the Muslim Brotherhood), and for the breakaway from it (the Iranian Revolution, Al-Qaeda).

Sunni pan-Islamism: from the Muslim Brotherhood to the Salafists

Sunni pan-Islamism underwent a remarkable shift in the second half of the 20th century. Embodied initially by the Muslim Brotherhood, it essentially defined itself as the Islamisation of pan-Arabism, embracing most of its goals (hostility towards Western neocolonialism and Israel, and the unification of the Arab world). From this perspective, the differences between Shi'ism and Sunnism among Arabs are completely secondary, as is the division of Sunnism into major legal schools. But from the 1980s, a new movement emerged, Salafism, which started in Saudi Arabia and Pakistan. Salafism was vehemently anti-Shia and anti-Communist (it would become anti-Western after the collapse of the USSR). Most importantly, it was pan-Islamist and not pan-Arab: Kashmir and Afghanistan were just as central as Palestine. And Salafism places the emphasis on *sharia* rather than the building of Islamic institutions. Today, this movement is dominant: it has absorbed a section of the Muslim Brotherhood, although the latter still exists at a national level in Egypt, Jordan, Palestine and Kuwait.

The Muslim Brotherhood comes under the banner of pan-Arabism. Its followers are Arabs and Sunnis. It supported nationalist movements (many members of the Egyptian Free Officers Movement supporting Nasser, like Anwar al-Sadat, had links with the Muslim Brotherhood), but very soon it found itself in competition with these movements. The Muslim Brotherhood was therefore repressed in all the republics, and was only able to continue to operate legally in the monarchies and emirates. But the situation varies enormously. In Syria, the struggle between the ruling powers and the Brotherhood was all the more violent because it was linked to a sectarian conflict between Sunnis and Alawites; consequently the Muslim Brotherhood was crushed as a result of massacres (Hama in 1982), mass arrests and exile. In contrast, while the Egyptian regime refused to recognise the Brotherhood as a political movement and was occasionally repressive (especially of course in Nasser's time), it allowed some room for manoeuvre: the Muslim Brotherhood was able to maintain its activities and put itself forward at elections from time to time in a variety of guises. In Saudi Arabia, an agreement between the monarchy and the organisation prohibited the Brotherhood from setting up a branch on Saudi territory in exchange for support overseas. In Jordan and Kuwait, the Muslim Brotherhood is legal and takes part in elections. In Palestine, it spawned Hamas. In Yemen, it has transformed itself into a political party (Islah), while in North Africa, the Muslim Brotherhood movement did not arrive until the 1980s.

Between 1950 and 1960, radicalism found an outlet in progressive secular movements. Nasser (described as a "new Hitler" in France during the Suez crisis of 1956) proclaimed himself the leader of pan-Arabism and clashed with the Saudis (on whom he waged a proxy war in Yemen from 1962 to 1967). In retaliation, the Saudis stepped up their support for pan-Islamist movements, above all to counter "progressive" Arab nationalism. For a brief period in the 1980s, the Israelis conducted a similar policy in Palestine that would lead to the emergence of Hamas. Similarly, for a time, dictatorships born of Arab nationalism (in Sadat's Egypt and also in Tunisia) fomented the rise of Islamist movements on campuses at the expense of left-wing groups. Support for the Afghan mujahideen can also be understood as a wish to use Islam against anything resembling "Marxism" in any shape or form. And on the other hand, it explains the Arab nationalists' great reluctance to support the Afghan resistance against the Soviets, who moreover were seen as allies in combating American "imperialism" and Zionism.

But the Saudis remained wary of the Muslim Brotherhood, which was too independent (and also critical of the Saudi monarchy). They developed their own pan-Islamist networks which were closer to Wahhabi circles, and in 1962 founded the World Islamic League (*Rabita Al 'Alam Al Islami*), whose stances are less political but tend to be pan-Islamist rather than pan-Arab. This fits into what I have termed the neo-fundamentalist line: do not raise the issue of the state but focus on *sharia*. Many members of the Muslim Brotherhood in exile found positions in the *Rabita* movement.

The success of the Iranian revolution of 1979 was a new direct threat to the Saudis. Khomeini saw the pro-American, "royalist" Saudis, who were Wahhabi and therefore violently anti-Shia, as the chief obstacle to the spread of the Islamic revolution in the Arab world. Unlike Saddam Hussein, they claimed religious legitimacy (control of the Holy Places). In fact, shortly after the Iranian revolution, the Saudi king proclaimed he was the "custodian of the two sanctuaries", in response to the Iranian argument that there is no king in Islam. The Saudis now had three enemies: Arab nationalism, Communism and Iranian Shi'ism. They would mobilise their neofundamentalist movement against Iran and therefore against the Shia.

The paradox is that the establishment of these networks automatically threatened all the enemies of Israel, the so-called refusal front. The Saudis of course do not like Israel, but nor do they have any real quarrel with the Jewish state. However they feel duty-bound to pronounce anti-Zionist rhetoric so as to remain credible, and many people who follow them are violently anti-Israel.

This Salafist movement has absorbed part of the Muslim Brotherhood. The two organisations embarked on "joint-ventures", like sending volunteers to Afghanistan, in the early 1980s. The story of the Palestinian Muslim Brother Abdullah Azzam, reputed to be Osama Bin Laden's ideological mentor, clearly indicates the turning point. Abdullah Azzam broke away from Yasser Arafat's PLO and its nationalism, also distancing himself from pan-Arabism, even in its Islamised form. Instead he advocated support for the Afghan resistance which embodied for him the true *ummah* for all Muslims, irrespective of ethnic origin and race. From this viewpoint, Palestine is just one jihad among many others, like Afghanistan, Chechnya and Kashmir. Another political trend bolstered this shift towards militant, internationalist "jihadism": it claimed to have started with Sayyid

Qutb, a Muslim Brother who in the late 1950s adopted a much harder line than that of the Brotherhood and was to become the intellectual leader of an entire radical jihadist movement which went beyond the Muslim Brotherhood.

This movement broke away from Saudi Arabia, becoming international as a result of its Afghan experience. It linked up with radical Pakistani, Malaysian, Indonesian and Central-Asian movements, and with young second-generation Muslims from Europe, as well as converts of all tendencies who all came together in Afghanistan. Pan-Arabism was superseded by a globalised pan-Islamism. That explains the movement's ability to make connections and become established in non-Arab circles, mainly in Pakistan and among immigrant Muslim communities in Europe.

On top of this Salafist Sunni movement's jihadism, there is a visceral anti-Shi'ism. The Muslim Brotherhood was not fundamentally anti-Shia, but rather saw Shiism as a fifth legal school of Islam. Its antipathy towards Khomeini was more political than religious. But the Wahhabis and Salafis consider Shi'ism as a heresy, and so fighting against the Iranian revolution is thus a religious obligation. And finally, anti-Shi'ism was strengthened by the influence of the Pakistani movements, with parties like the Sipah-e Saheba, set up to combat Shi'ism.

The Iranian revolution—between Islamic universality and Shia communities

Iran's Islamic revolution never claimed to be "Shia"; it always defined itself as the vanguard of the *ummah* of all Muslims. But the Iranian religious networks behind it and which served to export it abroad were essentially Shia. Likewise its ideology (millenarianism, the role of the imam, the concept of *vilayat-i faqih* or "guardianship of the Islamic jurists") is profoundly influenced by Shi'ism. This ambiguity is reflected in Islamic Iran's constitution which defines Twelver Shi'ism[4] as Iran's official religion but which makes the Supreme Leader of the Revolution the leader of the entire *ummah*, irrespective of different religious schools of thought. Shi'ism is thus implicitly presented as the most perfect form of Islam, which of course offended a large number of Sunnis, even among those who supported the revolution. Furthermore, the revolution first of all made an impact on the Shia populations, even if they were far from unanimous in their support. A certain number of prestigious Shia religious leaders everywhere (Khu'y in Iraq, Sham-

---

4   Twelver Shi'ism is the most prevalent school of thought among the Shia. It believes in twelve imams as successors to the Prophet, before the "occultation" of the twelfth imam (he disappeared but is not considered to be dead); the other main groups believe in five (Zaidi) or seven (Ismailis).

suddin in Lebanon) rejected the concept of *vilayat-i faqih*; others, while supporting the Islamic revolution, refused to recognise Khomeini's successors as spiritual guides (as in the case of Fadlallah in Lebanon).

In any case, the Islamic revolution led to the realignment and radicalisation of non-Iranian Shia populations. The revolution was not able to overcome the antagonism between Shi'ism and Sunnism; it even exacerbated it. In restoring a new universalist and radical dimension to Shi'ism, mobilising some of the Shia communities abroad and rejecting any structural alliance with the major Sunni Islamist movements (such as the Muslim Brotherhood, which did not necessarily want such a pact), the Iranian revolution revived the division between the two schools, although this was a result of the rift being instrumentalised by political and religious leaders rather than occurring spontaneously among the populations concerned. One paradox then is that the animosity between Shia and Sunnis, which seemed to wane in the Muslim world after the University of Al Azhar's *fatwa* of 1959 recognising Shi'ism as the fifth legal school of Islam (with the four major Sunni schools), witnessed a sudden escalation leading to armed confrontations in a number of countries (above all Pakistan, but also Lebanon and Afghanistan, and later Iraq).

A Tectonic Upheaval: Shia Against Sunnis: An Old Rivalry or a New Schism?

The conflict between Shia and Sunnis does not reflect an age-old battle for control of the Middle East and the Muslim world. Granted, the original split in the early days of Islam, after the death of the fourth caliph and successor of the Prophet (Ali), was originally political and not theological: must the Prophet's successor be a direct descendent, thus from his son-in-law Ali (as the Shia argued), or should he be chosen from among the community (the Sunni position)? At first, i.e. on the death of the Prophet, everyone was Arab by definition and the conflict was not between Arabs and Persians. The Shia lost from the outset, and definitively, after the battle of Karbala (680), the commemoration of which is one of the most important days in the Shia religious calendar. Subsequently, the minority Shia fell back on eschatology (waiting for the return of the twelfth imam), which distanced them from active political life. True, some dynasties (sometimes Arab, sometimes Persian) were Shia, or had Shia sympathies (like the Fatimids of Egypt or the Yemeni Zaydites). The Shia supported the Abbasid caliphs; a dynasty of Persian and Shia grand viziers at the palace (the Buyids) had considerable influence at the heart of the caliphate even though it had remained Sunni. Shi'ism only became a geostrategic factor once it was identified with the Iranian Empire from the time of the Safavid dynasty (1501-1727). The four empires vying for control of the Greater Middle East in the 16th and 17th centuries (Safavids, Ottomans, Uzbeks and Mughals on the Indian sub-continent) all belonged to the Turko-Persian civilisation. The first was Shia, the other three Sunni. Already, the Safavids were sending missionaries to their rivals (especially the Mughals), while the Ottomans were only too pleased to take over the high-ranking Shia clergy in Najaf after the fall of the Safavid dynasty to the Afghans (who came from the same Ghilzai confederation that would be the cradle of the Taliban two and a half centuries later). The boundary between the two spheres of influence was established, as mentioned above, by the Treaty of Qasr-i Shirin in 1639. The border between Iran and Afghanistan, determined in the 19th century, was also a dividing line between Shi'ism and Sunnism, not between ethnic-linguistic groups.

Shia-Sunni antagonism is not structural at the geostrategic level. It only comes into play when an actor (an empire or state) decides to play the faith card in order to delegitimise its adversary of the moment.

And so the Shia have ended up as a minority everywhere except in Iran. Nowhere do they hold political power and rarely do they constitute a homogeneous group. They are to be found in the international networks of clerics, which, from Najaf and Karbala, supply the urban *ulemas* (religious leaders) throughout the Middle East and the Indian sub-continent, and among the urban traders and middle classes, or just as equally in rural communities (south Lebanon), and sometimes tribal societies (southern Iraq). There have frequently been clashes between the two communities in the cities, especially during the Shia festival of Ashura (the commemoration of the battle of Karbala), but without that affecting the balance of power. The Shia did not participate as such in government, which remained Sunni, although they might have been recruited on an individual basis.

The 1960s onwards saw Shia communities asserting their identity in all the countries with a strong Shia minor-ity (which demographically may be the majority, as in Iraq), but it was only from the 1970s that they showed an interest in playing a role on the political stage. Often rural-dwell-ers (south Lebanon, the Bekaa valley, Punjab, Hazarajat in Afghanistan, the Alawites in Syria), the Shia were generally represented by traditional, sometimes tribal, leaders, and the urban Shia elite was out of touch with them. But from the 1970s, more or less everywhere, mullahs (such as Musa Sadr in Lebanon), supported by young intellectuals, ousted the traditional leadership and proclaimed the unity of the Shia community based on faith (demanding for example a specific fiscal and legal status taking "Jafarite law" into account). This movement predates the Islamic revolution in Iran (which, incidentally, was a party to it), but the 1979 revolution gave it a new lease of life and above all legitimacy. Splits and sometimes civil war among Shia (as in Afghanistan between 1983 and 1986) communities resulted in Shia political sectarianism.

Hezbollah is a good example of the complexity of such sectarian affirmation among one group. It is primarily the expression of a large section of the traditionally marginalised Lebanese Shia population. In this sense it is a community-oriented party. But Hezbollah then positioned itself as the Lebanese nationalist party: fighting the Israeli occupation and demanding Israel's withdrawal from the Shebaa farms area. Then on a third level, Hezbollah is part of a Middle-Eastern Shia axis, allying itself with Syria and Iran.

A specific case is that of the Syrian Alawites. They were a rural, despised *asabiyya* (solidarity group), which used the instruments of modernisation (the military academy, to be specific) to achieve a position of strength and seize power from the Sunni majority, which in turn became sectarian in opposition to them, especially since the only political challenge came from the Muslim Brotherhood. Suddenly, the Alawites, seeking outside support and religious legitimacy, obliterated their identity as a heretical sect, and some of them positioned themselves as Shia, both at the religious (obtaining *fatwas* from Lebanese or Iranian imams declaring them orthodox Muslims) and geostrategic level (alliances with Islamic Iran and Hezbollah in Lebanon).

Not all the Shia groups are fully aligned with Iran: the Iraqi Dawa party defined itself above all as Iraqi nationalist, and most of the grassroots Iraqi Shia remained loyal to Saddam Hussein during the war with Iran, even if their leaders took refuge in Tehran. After a period of keen interest in the Iranian revolution during the 1980s, the Shia of Arabia and the Gulf then sought recognition as stakeholders in a national process and effectively obtained an improvement in their situation.

Finally, the transnational networks of Shia clerics are divided over the significance of this transnationalism: is it primarily religious or political? The Lebanese leader Sheikh Fadlallah declared his political support for Iran's Islamic revolution but refused to recognise the *vilayat* [guardianship] of the current "Supreme Leader of the Revolution", Ayatollah Khamenei. The spiritual leader of the Iraqi Shia, Sistani, refuses to give Shi'ism as such a political dimension and nor does he support the Islamic revolution. Many Shia can simultaneously lay claim to the transnational nature of Shia religious identity and to a national political identity; this is true for example of the "Shirazis" (disciples of the Iranian Ayatollah Shirazi) in Bahrain and Kuwait.[5]

The Shia awakening and its instrumentalisation by Iran led to a very violent Sunni reaction, which was felt first of all in Pakistan and then spread to the entire Muslim world. In the 1980s, several radical groups, the most notorious being the Sepa-e Saheba,[6] encouraged by the Pakistani secret services (ISI), started routinely attacking prominent Shia figures and mosques in Pakistan. The Shia in turn formed armed groups. Within a few years, this sectarian war resulted in the end of Shia-Sunni cohabitation: each kept to their own areas, and the mosques in the south Punjab were turned into fortresses. The phenomenon extended to the rest of the Muslim world, without necessarily being as violent. Today, Azerbaijan is probably the only country where there are still mixed mosques and Shia and Sunnis pray together. So we are witnessing self-segregation along almost ethnic

5   See Laurence Louër, "Les reconfigurations du chiisme politique au Moyen Orient", in Rémy Leveau (ed.), *Afrique du Nord Moyen-Orient. Espace et conflits*, La documentation française, 2004.

6   See Mariam Abou-Zahab and Olivier Roy, *Islamist Networks: The Afghan-Pakistan Connection*, trans. John King, Hurst, 2004.

lines, which ceases to be purely a matter of Shia and Sunni religious identity. It is akin to the Northern Ireland model, where Protestants and Catholic are quasi-ethnic communities rather than religions.

Self-segregation, territorialisation, often accompanied by ethnic cleansing, the formation of self-defence militias which also carry out reprisal attacks: whatever the political or ideological facade, between 1984 and 2004, the Shia-Sunni split became a key feature of the Muslim world, from the Mediterranean to the Indus. North Africa, South-East Asia and Central Asia were not involved in this new division, for lack of significant numbers of Shia.

Shia and Sunnis in the Middle East: the new balance of power

Two events created a sea change in the balance of power between Shia and Sunnis: the Islamic revolution in Iran and the American military intervention in Iraq (2003). In the late 1980s, the Shia groundswell that had accompanied the Islamic revolution and which Iran had instrumentalised was contained and kept in check by the Sunni Arab states. Iran had effectively lost the war against Iraq, which demonstrated its role as the shield of the Arab Middle East against Iranian ambitions. True, the Lebanese Hezbollah, an ally of

Iran, had been granted recognition by the Taef Agreement on Lebanon (1989), but the central power in Beirut was still shared between Christians and Sunnis, paradoxically backed by Syria, the West and Saudi Arabia. In the 1990s, after a decade of strife and anti-Shia repression, the Gulf states, Bahrain, Kuwait and Saudi Arabia, began, in a controlled manner, to open up the political arena to their Shia citizens. As for Syria, whose regime is the creation of a sect close to Shi'ism, officially it always played the Arab nationalism card against Israel and the West. In Afghanistan, the Shia, too far removed from Iran, sided with Commander Massoud's Northern Alliance in 1992, then joined the US-backed Karzai government in 2002. Deprived of any territorial base, the Shia in Pakistan have not been able to play any part at national level. And in Yemen, the Zaydi Shia of the North—Shia sympathisers but not aligned with Iran—received Saudi backing against the Sunnis of the South, who are more liberal, socialist even, in the former South Yemen. What is more, the Zaydi are being wooed by Saudi Wahhabi-influenced Salafi movements—a completely unheard of example of Shia being "Sunni-ised").[7]

---

7   François Burgat, *Islamisme à l'heure d'al-Qaida*, La Découverte, 2005, pp. 32 ff.

This precarious equilibrium of the 1990s, which made it possible to come to terms with the impact of the Iranian revolution, was shattered by the American military intervention in Iraq. After 2003, in both Iraq and Lebanon, central power shifted to the Shia. Sunni Iraq disappeared, even though there is no guarantee that a stable central state will be formed around the Shia. In Lebanon, the national pact of 1943 provided for power-sharing between the faiths, essentially for the benefit of the Christians and the Sunnis (who respectively held the presidency and the post of prime minister, while the Shia only held the symbolic post of president of the national assembly). But Hezbollah's rise to power reached its peak after the short war of July 2006 against Israel. What Hezbollah wants is no more and no less than for the pact of 1943 to be overturned, but in its favour, or rather in favour of a new alliance, this time between Shia and Christians (hence the Maronite General Aoun's support for Hezbollah). The losers in Hezbollah's rise are not so much the Christians, who are in decline anyway, partly for demographic reasons, but the Sunnis. It is clear that Hezbollah is taking the Malay model rather than the Iranian: the Christians are not *dhimmis* ("protected"), but citizens who have their own legal system (for example, women are not subject to the obligation to wear the veil). On the other hand, the Sunnis must keep in line with the Shia, because of the fact that they are Muslim. In Syria, political power is in the hands of a non-Sunni group, the Alawites, who either define themselves as Shia or are aligned with Iran. The Kharijites of Oman, who historically have nothing to do with the Shia (for they do not recognise Ali, the key figure of Shi'ism, as the Prophet's successor), also differentiate themselves from the Sunnis.

In short, from the Mediterranean to Iran, the Sunnis to-day appear to be politically in a minority (Iraq, Lebanon, Syria), when they are not also in a minority demographically (Iraq, Lebanon, Bahrain, Oman). The fact is there are only two states east of Suez that remain solidly Sunni: Jordan and Saudi Arabia (plus a few of the Gulf emirates). This represents a tectonic upheaval which will have major repercussions. For many countries, the "Shia threat" will overshadow the Palestinian issue (Saudi Arabia, Jordan), and although the Shia Arabs are not necessarily pro-Iranian, they are perceived to be so by the Sunnis which may drive them into Iran's arms, or at least reinforce their sense of identity.

In this context, the execution of Saddam Hussein on the day of Eid ul Adha or Festival of Sacrifice, the commemoration of Abraham's sacrifice (31 December 2006), brutally underlined the division between the Shia, who openly rejoiced, and the Sunnis, who made him a hero of the Arab and Sunni cause (even the many Islamists who had criticised him in their time). The division immediately became a symbol that was etched in the popular memory. It is no longer a question of abstract geostrategic analysis but takes the concrete form of mutual hatred and rejection. It is conceivable that east of Suez, the division between Shia and Sunnis will become more fundamental than the conflict between Israel and the Palestinians.

Iraq: the inevitable partition, unless there is an implosion

Iraq's slide towards three separate entities (Kurdish, Shia and Sunni) is not simply the result of the increased violence. It is part of a much more profound process. Firstly, Kurdistan's march towards independence, begun in the 1970s, was effectively reinforced by having spent the years from 1991 to 2003 within the exclusion zone defined by the West to prevent Saddam Hussein's troops from advancing beyond the 36th parallel. Subsequently, the Kurds were naturally eager to be self-governed after Saddam Hussein's defeat, putting aside the long rivalry between the two parts of Kurdistan—the North with Barzani and the South with

Talabani. The Kurds then set out to win back the "Arabised" areas around Mosul and Kirkuk. But above all, more than fifteen years of isolation have transformed the Kurds' relationship to Iraq. Arabic is spoken less and less, no one wants to study in Baghdad any longer and mixed marriages are in freefall. In short, Kurdistan is automatically heading towards independence. The two neighbours, Turkey and Iran, are opposed to this independence, but are resigned to it in exchange for the guarantee that there will be no demands on their Kurds, which Barzani and Talabani will probably accept. Effectively, the two would lose all power in an enlarged Kurdistan that included the Kurds of Turkey, who are numerically superior and whose separatist organisation, the PKK, is more organised and, above all, little inclined to power sharing. But on the other hand, independent Iraqi Kurdistan, which is hemmed in, will need Turkey and Iran to exercise a sort of patronage to keep things on course. Which augurs occasional armed interventions by Turkey.

As for the Iraqi Shia and Sunni Arabs, the January 2006 elections show that the division is very deep. The result of the legislative elections confirms the territorialisation of different communities and therefore the inevitable slide towards federalism. People voted according to community allegiances, not political criteria, even in areas where there is no tension between the groups. But the electoral map also reveals the areas of conflict that would result from creating large, homogeneous regions. These are, of course, with one exception, the border areas between the three major emerging regions. To have a clearer picture, the electoral results of the 102 districts would need to be analysed, not just those of the 18 provinces.[8] First, of the 102 districts, 87 voted by a majority of at least two thirds for a homogenous ethnic-religious community coalition (Shia, Sunni, or Kurdish), 7 voted by an absolute majority for such a coalition (3 Shia, 3 Kurds and one Sunni) and only 8 voted along non-community lines. Just one of these 102 districts (Tell Afar, in the province of Nineveh) returned an absolute majority for a community-identified group (in this case Shia), even though it does not border on the overwhelmingly Shia territory of the south (it would appear that the Shia Arab vote was bolstered by that of the Shia Turkmens and the Yazidis a heterodox Kurdish sect). Everywhere else, it is the areas of contact (and the capital) which remain heterogeneous. So there are three massive territorial areas with a territorial band of friction. It is within this band that most of the

8   We refer here to the map of electoral results drawn up by the United Nations office in Baghdad.

bombings occur, which will lead to its being turned into a border, following the exodus of minority populations.

Unsurprisingly, the districts divided between Shia and Sunni occupy all the provinces of Dyala (except the district furthest north, which is overwhelmingly Sunni) and Baghdad. The other "mixed" districts are along the boundary of the autonomous Kurdish region. So there are two areas of tension: between Shia and Sunnis around Baghdad, extending east to the Iranian border, and between Kurds and Sunnis along the Mosul-Kirkuk-Khanaqin axis. Moreover, all three groups are present in Tell Afar, to the west of Mosul: this last flashpoint is important as it is on the border and can involve Turkey and Syria.

As for the area of friction between the Kurdish region and the Sunni Arab area, the tension is heightened by the continuous advance of the Kurds to the west of the green line (defining the autonomous Kurdish region of 1991), which is happening in two ways: the return of the Kurdish population and therefore the expulsion of Arabs, and the role of the Peshmerga militia in maintaining order. The areas where the tension is particularly high are east of Mosul and around Kirkuk.

The question is: will the openly federalist constitution alleviate these tensions, for it deliberately contains profound ambiguities? It does not define the regions but stipulates that the provinces can be grouped in regions or not. As power is devolved to the regions rather than the provinces, there is a strong incentive to form regional groupings, but the methods are vague and consider only the provinces as actors, not the districts. The constitution says nothing about the districts being permitted to change province in order to be in a region closer to their choice of community affiliation (especially when they are on the border).

In eight Shia provinces in the south, three Kurdish (Suleymaniye, Dahuk, Erbil) and two Sunni (Al Anbar, Salaheddin), the creation of homogeneous, autonomous regions will not be problematic. But in the provinces of Nineveh, At Taymin, Dyala, Baghdad and Babil, a certain number of districts will reject the province's majority choice. Then what will happen? If there is no constitutional solution, after a period of local conflicts, it will probably be necessary to re-draw the administrative boundaries on the basis of local referendums, or to allow exchanges of populations to go ahead, and even endorse forms of ethnic cleansing. It is also likely that militias will set out from the territorial bastions to help their brothers in the disputed areas (which the Kurds are already doing, and which the Sunnis have started doing with the suicide bombings against the Shia).

The conflicts will therefore lead to groupings along community lines with the flight of minority populations or those whose militia have been defeated locally. The phenomenon of polarisation and territorialisation along community lines is self-perpetuating.

But there is also a gloomier scenario: the impossibility of a true community-centred grouping because of intra-community conflicts. These can arise either out of essentially tribal, traditional segmentation, or from recompositions as a result of the war, in the form of militias ruled by local leaders, whether they claim religious affiliations or are simple local "gangs". The violent battle that took place near Najaf on 28 and 29 January 2007 between the US-backed Iraqi army and a curious alliance between a Shia tribe (the Hawatem), which wanted to avenge the assassination of its chief by the Iraqi army, and a millenarianist Shia sect (the "Soldiers of Heaven") is a good illustration of the complex interconnection between traditional segmentation and new forms of radicalisation. Similarly, as well as being a political movement, Sheikh Moqtada al-Sadr's militia is also a sect and a mafia gang. In the north, the alliances between Sunni tribes and Al-Qaeda groups are reversible. This breakdown of political movements into *asabiyya* and the recomposition of traditional *asabiyya* around "contemporary" issues

115

(ideologies, the economic market, international alliances, globalisation) are a constant in contemporary local conflicts where civil war goes hand in hand with foreign intervention (Afghanistan, Lebanon, Chechnya, not to mention Africa).

Iran between two fronts

Iran's objective is to be the dominant power in the Middle East, and in particular to acquire a sort of patronage over the Gulf States. Iran is playing two cards: the Shia axis in the Gulf and the Israel refusal front—in other words, Arab nationalism and pan-Islamism. However the two are contradictory. Meanwhile Iran's nuclear programme fulfils two purposes: to constitute an instrument of power in a Middle East that has at least two nuclear powers (Pakistan and Israel), and to safeguard its territory from any threat coming from the United States or Israel. Iran may negotiate, suspend its nuclear activities or stop on the threshold of carrying out nuclear tests (following the example of Israel), but it will not abandon its nuclear programme, i.e. halt uranium enrichment. The American military intervention in the wake of 9/11 was a remarkable opportunity for Iran, now rid of its two enemies: Saddam Hussein and the Taliban.

Iran learned lessons from its failure to export the revolution and from the war with Iraq in the 1980s. It needs to smash the front between Arab nationalists, Sunni militants and conservative monarchies that has resulted in its isolation. To do so, Iran is trying to assume leadership of the refusal front, the opposition to the state of Israel, through Hezbollah, at a time when Arab regimes are endorsing the existence of the Jewish state. That is the motive behind Ahmadinejad's aggressive declarations about wiping Israel from the map and his denial of the Holocaust. Even if the outbreak of war between Hezbollah and Israel in July 2006 appears to be a misguided initiative on the part of Hezbollah, which underestimated Israel's reaction to the kidnapping of two Israeli Defence Force soldiers, the fact is that the outcome played into Tehran's hands. From Cairo to Amman, the Arab populace see Hassan Nasrallah, general secretary of Hezbollah, as an Arab hero.

Even if in the view of a number of Iranian leaders Ahmadinejad goes too far, his approach is logical: delegitimise the Gulf monarchies and defuse Shia-Sunni tensions by emerging as the leader of the Arab cause. It is therefore in Iran's interest for all the conflicts in the region to be interconnected, by bringing together the refusal front (essentially Arab) and the "Shia axis". At the same time, open war between Shia and Sunnis in Iraq is to be avoided, for Iran would be forced to intervene, which would mean confronting Saudi Arabia, directly or indirectly, and that would damage its standing among the Sunni Arab populations of the Near East (Egypt, Palestine, Jordan, Syria, and even North Africa). Iran therefore has no wish to see the Americans leave Iraq too soon, for Islam's internecine conflict would only be exacerbated and affect the wider region. Therefore to have the Americans bogged down in Iraq is the best option for Tehran.

Iran is playing the Shia card in Iraq, but has no intention on concentrating on it such that it risks falling back into the Shia ghetto and being confronted once more with an alliance between Arab nationalists, conservative monarchies and Sunni militants. The refusal front and the "Shia axis" are, in fact, contradictory, even if they are tactically used together by Iran. That is why it is in Iran's interest to step up the pressure while avoiding an open military confrontation.

This contradiction is also evident in Al-Qaeda's attitude, which is the only organisation that, like Iran, has a presence on all fronts. In Iraq and Afghanistan, the organisation has taken the anti-Shia line. But to emphasise the division between Shia and Sunnis is to weaken the anti-Israel and anti-Western front. That is why the leadership of Al-Qaeda was concerned that prior to his death in June 2006, Zarqawi, the head of the organisation he called "Al Qaeda in Iraq", was prioritising the fight against the Shia.

As a result, the Iranians are attempting a tactical rapprochement with Sunni radicals (in 2007, for example, they were negotiating discreetly with the Taliban in Quetta, in south west Pakistan). But the repeated attacks against the Iranian security forces in the province of Seistan (home to the Sunni Baluchis) show that radical Sunni groups, probably linked to local drug traffickers and the Pakistani security services, do not see things in the same light. The alliance that supported the Afghan mujahideen in the 1980s (Saudi Arabia, Pakistan, radical Sunni groups) is reforming, with probably the same pernicious effects: a radicalisation that eludes the control of its promoters (it is this movement that spawned Al-Qaeda). At the same time, the conservative Sunni states feel more threatened by Iran than by Israel and so have distanced themselves from Hezbollah.

The question is how the Salafist movement will develop in relation to Shi'ism. It all depends on the battlefield. While joint actions cannot be ruled out, especially in the event of an American attack on Iran, in Iraq we are witnessing a new alliance between Arab nationalism and Salafism: thousands of Sunni Arab volunteers went to the "Sunni triangle" of Iraq. Even if initially they crossed the border to fight the Americans, they inevitably find themselves caught up in the escalating tensions between Shia and Sunnis. The Wahhabis and many Salafis continue to see the Shia as heretics,[9] whereas those close to the Muslim Brotherhood regard the differences between Shia and Sunnis as secondary to their shared aims, as Yussuf Qaradawi reminded the Brotherhood's members after the war between Israel and Hezbollah.

Hezbollah is the key to unlocking the connection between the two axes. It has clearly demonstrated its community-oriented and national choices (defence of both the Lebanese Shia and of a "recomposed" Lebanon), yet is not an unalienable ally of Tehran. It all depends too on the American reaction towards Iran. If the latter goes too far, it can lose everything. True, attacks against American interests may be carried out, but the established movements (Hamas, Hezbollah, Dawa in Iraq) have nothing to gain in playing the politics of disruption. Furthermore, many Iranian conservatives believe that Ahmadinejad has already overstepped the mark. The Iranian factor is therefore one of the keys to the evolution of the crisis.

---

9   In Dec. 2006 a conference convened in Istanbul in support of the Iraqis brought together only Sunnis, one off whom, the Saudi Sheikh Nasir Bin Sulayman al-Umar, called on Sunnis to unite against the Shia.

3

IRAN POISED BETWEEN THE
NUCLEAR BOMB AND BOMBARDMENT

The Iranian nuclear question is complex. While no one knows when Iran will have a fully-fledged nuclear bomb, the perception that it has one is a deterrent in itself; there is no need for it to conduct nuclear tests. Above all, there is a profound ambiguity in the West concerning the definition of the threat. There is a consensus that it is unacceptable for Iran to have access to a military nuclear programme, but in what way is a nuclear Iran threatening? There are two answers to this question, each requiring a different policy. The first identifies the regime as the problem: an Islamic republic would be tempted to use the bomb against Israel or to use the fact that it has the bomb to create a sanctuary for terrorist groups on its soil. This is the position of the Bush administration. The second view is that the deterrent will function irrespective of the regime and that the problem is rather that if Iran were allowed to achieve its nuclear ambitions, this would have a proliferation effect, since Egypt, Saudi Arabia and Turkey would then go nuclear. Iran is also a signatory to the Non-Proliferation Treaty (unlike India, Pakistan and Israel) so its withdrawal would mean the death of the NPT. The regime in power in Tehran makes little difference. This is the dominant European view.

The strategy to be pursued depends on which view one subscribes to: in the first case, there needs to be a push for regime change; in the second, it is Iran as a regional nuclear power that is the problem. Hence a choice has to be made: should the focus be the regime or the nuclear programme?

It is a game of poker. The hardliners in Tehran do not believe that an American military strike is likely, and think that Iran's capability to retaliate on several fronts (Iraq primarily, but also Lebanon, Afghanistan, the Gulf, with terrorism targeting American military and economic objectives) is such that the US cannot risk an escalation. Meanwhile on the American side, it is difficult for President Bush, who was re-elected in 2004 because of his uncompromising stance in the battle against "global terrorism", to end his term on a note of failure (Iraq) and weakness (Iran). Throughout 2007, the Americans therefore ratcheted up the pressure, as if to prepare global public opinion for an aerial strike against Iran's nuclear facilities.

The question is complicated by the fact that a policy of escalating economic sanctions to compel Iran to halt its uranium enrichment programme (the Europeans' policy since 2003) has a slim chance of success, even if Iran is cunning and buys time by slowing down its programme. Sanctions will only be effective if backed up by a belligerent stance (the threat of attack). This was the line adopted by President Bush in 2007 (including detaining Iranian officials in Iraq, menacing rhetoric and confrontation with Moqtada al-Sadr's militia and cadres in Iraq), while organising an economic stranglehold on Iran without seeking a Security Council resolution (owing to the reluctance of Russia and China). The major international banks ceased dealing with Iran following discreet American pressure.

This policy has been successful in influencing Iranian conservative pragmatists like Rafsanjani, who believe that Iran could have achieved its objectives by avoiding confrontation. Here, the issues are Ahmadinejad's call to wipe Israel off the map and the Holocaust denial conference held in Tehran at the end of 2006.

There is no fundamental disagreement within the Iranian political establishment over Iran's ambition to be a major power, its need to have a nuclear capability, or over its ambition to weaken the Arab front. The argument is over the means.

In its trial of strength with Washington, Iran has one ace up its sleeve: the removal of Ahmadinejad from office, which is constitutionally possible. It is hard to imagine the United States bombing Iran immediately after the dismissal of the President followed by the announcement of presidential elections. And so it is important here to analyse Iran's political game.

The conservative camp is increasingly divided, even among the entourage of Ayatollah Khameni, the only person who can dismiss the president. There are the beginnings of a shift towards the moderates, led by Rafsanjani. In December 2006, the Iranian parliament, even though it is conservative, voted for the principle of curtailing the president's mandate. Articles hostile to Ahmadinejad have appeared in the conservative press. Above all, in the election of the Assembly of Experts, which elects the Supreme Leader of the Revolution, and in the local elections of December 2006, radical conservatives suffered a severe setback. All this indicates that the president has lost a great deal of support among the Supreme Leader's inner circle. Many conservatives already appear to have joined the pragmatists' camp, for a number of reasons. Firstly, the fear of economic sanctions: Iran's economy, which is undergoing a structural crisis, is in an even worse state under the presidency of Ahmadinejad, chiefly due to the threats of sanctions and the President's inept economic policy. The stock exchange is plummeting; petrol is rationed, capital is already haemorrhaging and foreign investment has dried up. The new middle class, having accumulated its wealth through speculation and protectionism, wants to be able to invest. Discontent has now spread across the social spectrum. The fear of an unbridled escalation in the Near East is another factor. Time is on Iran's side: given that the Americans will eventually leave, what is the point of risking a strike by raising the stakes? Yet President Ahmadinejad has steadily ignored calls for a more moderate stand and has, on the contrary, toughened his attitude, as shown by the sacking of Ali Larijani as the main negociator on the nuclear issue.

THE AHMADINEJAD PHENOMENON: A GLITCH OR PART OF A CONTINUUM?

Although the defeat of the reformists in Iran's presidential election of June 2005 came as no surprise, no one on the other hand had expected Mahmoud Ahmadinejad to be elected. In the first round, he obtained around 20% of the votes, which corresponds to the ideological core of the electorate mobilised by the clerical and political networks that had selected him as their candidate. This election does not therefore represent a conservative landslide, but means that the modernisers are running out of steam, unable either to break away from the regime or to transform it from within. In the second round, the Iranians voted principally against former president Akbar Hashemi-Rafsanjani, perceived less as a pragmatist than as the representative of the *nouveau riche* class—one of those men who had made a fortune thanks to the Islamic regime while urging Iranian citizens to practise self-denial and religious observance.

Once elected, the former mayor of Tehran chose not to devote himself solely to issues on which he had campaigned. On the contrary, he concentrated mainly on foreign policy by choosing confrontation over the two most sensitive issues for the international community: the nuclear programme and Israel. True, there is nothing new in the refusal to recognise the Jewish state or the determination to pursue a nuclear programme without ruling out the military option (these two stances were already in evidence under the presidency of the liberal Khatami); the deliberate choice of provocation does however mark one more milestone in bringing Iran into a phase of conflict with the West.

On the domestic front, the president's first decision was to proceed with the replacement—unprecedented since the revolution—of senior cadres in every sphere, so as to place his men in strategic positions. One sign of political wisdom, however, was that the new regime did not embark on the restoration of a crumbling moral and puritanical order which had been dented by the emergence of a young generation openly hostile to Islamic standards. And while it was expected that he would return to a certain economic orthodoxy once in power, the Iranian president attempted to fulfil his vote-winning election promises to support the working classes (as is borne out by his appeal to lower interest rates even though inflation was rising). And this in a context where the fulfilment of these promises is all the more problematic, given the crippling effect of the sanctions progressively imposed by the UN and the Americans from 2006 on an economy that is structurally ailing, despite oil revenues. Ahmadinejad seemed convinced that everything would be settled in the short term and that the external crisis would enable him to avert an internal crisis. Here, it is no coincidence that he draws on the millenarianist inspiration of the Islamic revolution, long since abandoned by the old political hands.

To try to understand the Ahmadinejad phenomenon, we must first examine the networks that brought him to power. He was first and foremost the candidate of the Pasdarans (Revolutionary Guards) and of the Bassijis (volunteer militia): these two bodies represent the hardliners of the regime and are probably the best organised political camp. In actual fact, there has never been a real political party in Islamic Iran. Khomeini himself disbanded his Islamic Republic Party immediately after his election victory. What is known today in Iran as "Hezbollah" (Party of God) is not a party but a generic term describing those who gravitate around the Bassijis and the Pasdarans.

Electoral campaigns see volatile coalitions form around a man and a programme; this was especially true during the two elections of Mohammed Khatami to the presidency, in 1997 and 2001. Moreover, these purely political coalitions are closely bound up with networks of personal relations, especially religious networks of mullahs who studied together under the authority of an ayatollah. The master-student relationship can last for several generations and be reinforced by family ties. These networks easily transcend purely political allegiances, but, when the two coincide, they have considerable power since their members have ready access to the Supreme Leader of the Revolution, whose office has become the true centre of power in Iran.

The other networks are those involving the Revolutionary Guards. This body is a paramilitary institution which constitutes a real parallel army (it even has a navy and an air force). The Guards, or Pasdarans, hold the reins of the foundations which have considerable funds at their disposal. There is often a lack of transparency as to how these funds are managed as they are governed neither by commercial law nor by public finance. A good number of Pasdarans have been implicated in financial scandals. Nor is the movement immune from in-fighting and personality clashes, if only because the young recruits do not necessarily have the same deep-rooted ideological convictions as their elders. But the *esprit de corps* works. The Pasdarans also control the Bassijis, made up of young men acting as a vigilante vice squad and serving as a "militant reserve force" for the regime. From the lower classes, puritanical both out of conviction and as a result of being excluded from a consumer society which they see as remaining the prerogative of the middle-class districts of north Tehran, the Bassijis are probably the last remnants of a revolution reduced to a populist and moral order. Furthermore, the Bassijis are supervised by some of the most ideological mullahs.

To put it plainly, the system operates through a vast network of nepotism, clientelism and social protectionism, sustained by oil revenues and income from the foundations. Furthermore, the Pasdarans have gone into business: in 2004, they closed the new Tehran airport, supposedly for security reasons. The real justification for their action was very different: the operating company appointed to run the airport was Turkish and a competitor of a Pasdaran owned business. By thus mixing economic nepotism and ideological "purity", the Pasdarans can mobilise a sufficient electoral base to tip the elections in their favour, especially when moderate sections of the electorate abstains. This is precisely what happened in the most recent presidential election.

Alliance with the clergy

Born in 1956, Ahmadinejad is the product of a new generation formed not by the struggle against the Shah's regime but by the war against Iraq (1980-1988). He studied to be an engineer but only obtained his doctorate in 1987, when he was already occupying an official position. The new president is a perfect example of those "Islamist engineers" who made up the backbone of fundamentalist movements throughout the Muslim world. What is specific to Iran (and which largely explains the success of the revolution) lies in the alliance between these militants from a secular background and a section of the clergy.

To be specific, Ahmadinejad has close ties to Ayatollah Mohammed Taqi Mesbah Yazdi. Born in 1935, Mesbah Yazdi is now the voice of the "revolutionary conservatives" among the clergy. He belongs to the generation that was mobilised in the 1950s as part of the Hojattieh Society, officially set up to fight against the Bahá'í,[1] but the organisation also opposed the power of the Shah. He was close to Ayatollah Seyyed Mohammad Hosseini Beheshti, Khomeini's first designated heir who was assassinated in 1981, with whom he established the Haqqani seminary in Qom to train the future cadres of the Islamic regime. This establishment combines a religious education with modern secular training, the idea being to give secular graduates from state universities a religious education and to give the clergy training in social sciences.

Ahmadinejad's advisor is a member of the Assembly of Experts (which elects the Supreme Leader). Even if Yazdi

---

1   A dissident religious Shia Islamic group which appeared in Iran in the mid-19th century, and which almost became the dominant minority religion before being persecuted. The struggle against the Bahá'í was revived in the 1950s by the clergy, who suspected the Shah of leniency towards them.

has no other official functions, he is an influential figure. Some of those close to him and his former students were at the head of the secret services. Extremely hostile towards the West, he is the first senior figure to have publicly endorsed a military nuclear programme. Both a religious conservative and a political radical, he has revised the messianic aspect of the revolution, which helps explain why the subject of the return of the hidden imam (or twelfth imam, descendent and representative of the Prophet, concealed since his disappearance in 873, who will return to earth to bring justice) should suddenly be topical again. Ahmadinejad referred to the twelfth imam in his speech of 16 November 2005 at the Friday assembly of imams. On several occasions, the president has claimed to have divine inspiration (such as during his address before the UN General Assembly, in September 2005); until now, such intense personal religiosity was not a characteristic of Iranian leaders who tend to be political rather than mystic.

Mesbah Yazdi is a great proponent of the theory of *vilayat-i faqih* (guardianship of the Islamic jurists) and considers that the will of the Leader should take precedence over the will of the people. He therefore refutes the idea that the Leader must renounce his powers for the revolution to have a democratic outcome.

This network of clerics includes other eminent figures such as Ayatollah Jannati, president of the Guardian Council, which is responsible for ensuring that the laws passed by Parliament comply with Islam, and for endorsing electoral candidates—a prerogative which allows this body to block Parliament, and even to control it indirectly. It is these connections with the clergy that smoothed Ahmadinejad's entry into the entourage of the Supreme Leader, Ali Khamenei, and gained their support. But his having been so ordained is not sufficient to explain his rise.

The influence of the Pasdarans

The second key to Ahmadinejad's success is the Pasdaran corps, which he joined in 1985. After participating in military operations in Iraqi Kurdistan, he left the front line to take charge of logistics. He definitely had connections to the secret services, even if there is no proof of his collaboration in the murder of members of the Kurdish opposition in Europe (here too, there is an inevitable parallel with Putin).

The Iraq war veterans' generation still holds the key positions, while those who became radicalised under the Shah are growing older and often become pragmatic, even liberal—like Akbar Ganji, one of the ringleaders of the American embassy hostage-taking operation in 1979. The conservatives' leaders among the clergy have been in place since the beginning of the revolution. As hardly any new revolutionary mullahs have emerged, it is the secular figures who are now taking over. These veterans "have a hold" on the Pasdarans, the Bassijis and the security services. Their figurehead is Ali Larijani, who is leader of the National Security Council and was till October 2007 Iran's chief nuclear negotiator. Larijani is a former Revolutionary Guard, as are his brother Mohammed Jawad, director of the Research Institute for Theoretical Physics and Mathematics, and Mojtaba Hashemi Samareh, Ahmadinejad's closest adviser. But Ali Larijani seems to have distanced himself from Ahmadinejad and is advocating negotiations with the West.

Many members of this generation are not acquainted with the outside world and see Iran as a fortress under siege—both culturally and militarily—from an America bent on eliminating the Islamic regime. Their actions have sometimes been compared with China's Cultural Revolution: a second revolutionary wind that blows twenty years after the initial revolution. Another common factor is the Supreme Leader's appeal to the country's "youth" to help him remove both his old-guard rivals (Rafsanjani) and the reformers. And one last factor for these veterans of the war against Iraq, as far as foreign policy is concerned, is the determination to avenge the "defeat" of 1988, a defeat they attribute to the coalition of Arab conservative regimes and Western powers.

Lack of uniformity

Here again, it is a question of networks and not a party: the "veterans" are not a uniform group. This generation has been in control of Parliament since the legislative elections of 2004. Lacking in experience and nearly a third of them Pasdarans, so far the deputies have distinguished themselves neither for their competence nor their political aptitude. While they are as keen to court public opinion as Mahmoud Ahmadinejad (refusal to authorise foreign investments, wariness towards privatising the economy, which must remain in the hands of the state, and therefore of the people, rather than the new middle class), they do however regularly oppose the President: they have, for example, objected to several of the candidates he presented for the post of Oil Minister, as well as his proposed draft budget, and voted to curtail his mandate.

And that is one of the paradoxes of Iran: the Constitution is taken seriously, and each branch of the government insists on its prerogatives. The rural deputies and particularly those from the medium-sized towns (which are experiencing a population explosion, whereas Tehran is stagnating) are discontented with Tehran's centralism and political supremacy. As for the city's new mayor, Mohammed Bagher Ghalibaf (born in 1961), a Pasdaran general and therefore also a veteran of the war against Iraq, he is known for his frosty relations with his predecessor. In short, the more Ahmadinejad seeks greater presidential autonomy and freedom of manoeuvre, the more he comes up against rival networks of all political stripes seeking to discredit him in the eyes of the Supreme Leader.

An anti-imperialist policy

Finally, it is impossible to understand Ahmadinejad's policies without taking into account its Third-Worldist and radical nationalist dimension which places Iran alongside Cuba, Venezuela and Bolivia in structural opposition to what is perceived as "American imperialism", as illustrated by Ahmadinejad's trip to Latin America in January 2007. It should be remembered that the Iranian revolution was as much anti-imperialist as Islamic.

But the promises of revolutionary Islam—social justice and economic development—have not been fulfilled. The salaried middle classes have been impoverished. Iran has found itself isolated from the international community.

Nationalism, very much alive, has become rooted in the certainty that for two centuries the country has been the victim of a plot hatched by the West, and therefore any event is seen as a manifestation of this conspiracy. Tehran's Holocaust denial is part of this paranoid reasoning: far from being the expression of grassroots anti-Semitism, it is in fact chiefly imported from Europe. Traditionally, the Muslim countries have considered Israel as a colonial state supported by a Europe that has passed the guilt it feels for the genocide of the Jews onto the Palestinians. But presenting the Holocaust as a myth—the founding myth of the State of Israel—is to echo the arguments of European holocaust deniers such as Roger Garaudy, which are very popular among the ruling elite. This type of anti-Zionism is also widespread among Iranian intellectuals closer to the far left than to Islamism—former members of the Tudeh Communist Party in particular. Let us not forget that they supported the regime because of its anti-imperialism.

WILL AMERICA BOMB IRAN?

What would be the impact were America to bomb Iran? In the short term, a tougher nationalist stance, an intensification of fighting on the three fronts where Western troops are involved (Iraq, Afghanistan, Lebanon)—and in doing so Iran would have no hesitation in forming alliances with its former enemies: the Salafi Sunnis, the Taliban and Al-Qaeda—and finally, an attempt to foment an oil crisis by directly or indirectly halting production and the movement of oil tankers in the Gulf. Iran will present itself as the victim of imperialism and Zionism, and the people will take to the streets to demonstrate their support for this champion of the resistance, while a series of terrorist acts are committed (in the West too) in retaliation for the bombing. Tehran will activate the first wing, the refusal front—and not Shia against Sunni.

In the long term, the scenario is more complex. Iran risks isolation. An international terrorist campaign will be counter-productive, unlike that of 1984-1986, which forced the West to quit Lebanon and tone down its support for Saddam Hussein. For since 9/11, terrorism is no longer seen as a tactical move but rather as a global threat. An American bombing attack on Iran would not create a sacrosanct sense of anti-American unity in Iraq, but would exacerbate the tensions. The Sunni Arab regimes would support American efforts to control the Persian Gulf, re-establish the movement of oil and regulate the market. In short, the Shia-Sunni division would continue on its own course. Neither Hezbollah, nor Hamas, nor Syria will launch into an escalation that would be contrary to their interests (even though they may consider it to their advantage to capitalise on the crisis with Iran to raise the stakes, which might lead to an unchecked escalation, particularly between Syria and Israel). On the other hand, it will be impossible for the Americans to leave Iraq, which will be plunged further into civil war. The Taliban will step up their offensives in Afghanistan to force the Pakistani government to make concessions in the face of frenzied public opinion and will divert Islamic militancy to the Afghan cause. As for Lebanon, like Palestine, it will have to make the choice it has been avoiding from the beginning: either an uncertain war against Hezbollah and Hamas, or a reconfiguration of Lebanon around Hezbollah, abandoning the option of an alliance with Iran and negotiation with Hamas, which has never been dependent on external alliances.

Iran is therefore the key to the current situation in the Middle East, but the risk is that neither Iran nor Saudi Arabia will be able to rein in the forces that the two countries have helped unleash. Neither the pan-Islamist radicalisation nor the division between Shia and Sunnis can be controlled by state strategies or by a return to a *Realpolitik* such as that advocated by the Baker report. And yet, now there is no other choice but to try and dissociate the conflicts, for example by including Hezbollah in regional negotiations together with Syria, and by opening a dialogue with Hamas. Either Iran is successfully isolated by military strikes and the repression of Shia activists in Iraq (and success is far from guaranteed), or negotiationns with Iran must take place. This can only happen if relations between Israel and the Palestinians improve so that Iran can no longer rely on the support of the refusal front. And yet, independently of the good or ill will of the actors, the two-state concept (Israeli and Palestinian) has today been superseded by the situation on the ground (Israeli settlements, Palestinian civil war). But at all events, the concept of the global war on terror must be abandoned because it does not make sense and leads to the wrong perceptions and policies.

4

In the Meantime, Al-Qaeda...

While the Americans are becoming mired in Iraq, Al-Qaeda is flourishing. If the West has taken a while to grasp the nature of Al-Qaeda, it is because it persisted, and many still persist, in seeing it as a territorialised, Middle East organisation of mainly Arabs bent on expelling the Christians and Jews from the Middle East in order to create a *dar ul-Islam* (Land of Islam), under the umbrella of a caliphate. They draw on the scholarly writings of classical Islam and the works of the 20th-century radicals like Sayyid Qutb to bring Al-Qaeda into the realm of the comprehensible, i.e. the past.

It was only with the London bomb attacks in July 2005 that the phenomenon of home-grown terrorism was glimpsed, without the consequences being grasped, since an organisation of Al-Qaeda's nature is still too often defined as the radical vanguard of the Muslim community in general. The issue then becomes the link between this "Muslim wrath" and terrorism: either the violence is seen as a desperate response to a Western aggression that is both territorial and cultural, or it is seen as the vanguard of a conquering Islam that is jihadist by definition.

But, as I argued in *Globalised Islam*, Al-Qaeda is in essence a deterritorialised, global organisation, relatively distanced from Middle East issues, with no political roots in the Muslim populations. It recruits chiefly among the "born again" on the fringes. But these fringes are not to be taken in the socioeconomic sense. In fact, Al-Qaeda's radicals are "de-territorialised": most of the time, their country of birth, the place of radicalisation and the place of action are not the same. The World Trade Center pilots and other terrorist suspects apprehended since 9/11, including in Britain, have had international career paths. It is pointless thinking of Al-Qaeda as a political organisation seeking to conquer and rule a territory. Al-Qaeda's strategy is twofold: it wants to confront the big boys, or rather *boy*, directly, striking out against America's power, relying not on the actual damage inflicted (financial cost, number of dead) but on image, media impact and the terror effect. And secondly it seeks to hijack existing conflicts and give them a new significance by making them part of the global jihad against the West. The mirror effect with the partisans of the clash of civilisations of course intensifies the impact. In fact, Al-Qaeda needs those who demonise it, for once again acknowledgement leads to political action.

But is Al-Qaeda a fringe organisation? Here the word "fringe" should be understood in every sense of the word. It has been said over and over again: Al-Qaeda's cadres' jihad of choice was in Afghanistan, Bosnia, Chechnya and Kashmir, where its activists were trained and the personal networks that were to become be the organisation's backbone were formed. Palestine is constantly referred to, it is true, but in the same way as the other struggles. Very few activists have been to the Israeli-Palestine theatre of operations (two as far as I know, assuming they are members of al-Qaeda), whereas far-left Western activists, such as the Baader-Meinhof gang and even the Japanese Red Army made it their priority. Similarly, whereas splinter groups such as that of Abu Nidal concentrated on Jewish or Israeli targets, Al-Qaeda, without forgetting the latter (Casablanca, Istanbul), focuses on "global" targets (major cities, financial centres, public transport), which reflects its determination to be seen as a global threat to the West and not as the agent of intercommunal regional warfare in which the ordinary Westerner would feel uninvolved.

Furthermore, for the youths who join Al-Qaeda or the current jihad, it is a means of breaking away. Breaking away from the family, their environment, their country of origin or their host country. No member of Al-Qaeda recruited in Europe has returned to fight in their family's country of origin (apart from a few Pakistanis), all have adopted an extreme version of Salafism, breaking away from their family's more traditional Islam. Nearly all enjoyed a very Westernised lifestyle before suddenly switching to a strict religious piety. The transition to violent action follows very quickly after the return to religion or conversion. It is striking to note that with each terrorist who is killed or arrested, the reaction of their family and neighbours is one of disbelief (unlike that towards Palestinian or Chechen suicide bombers). Since the London suicide bombings, the inevitable media visit to the family emphasises how assimilated the young man was, dating girls, drinking etc., until the day when... Nearly all the terrorists effectively become "born again" in the West and rediscover Islam at the mosque or, with increasing frequency, under the influence of a local "guru" like Farid Benyettou, a twenty-three year old self-proclaimed imam, arrested in January 2005, who recruited a group of young people from the Cité Curial housing estate in Paris's 19th *arrondissement* to go to fight in Iraq.

This fringe has no defining social profile: people from all social and economic backgrounds gravitate towards Al-Qaeda (even if they are not formally members of the organisation). They are not necessarily the bitter young unemployed, or victims of racism. Many are also the offspring of mixed-race couples: Jamal Loizeau, who died in Afghanistan in November 2001, Hakil Chraibi, a twenty-three year old student in Montpellier who left for Falluja in 2006, or Karim Mejjati, one of the suspected ringleaders of the network that carried out the Madrid attack in 2004. We should note here that militants who travel from one Middle Eastern country to fight in another, without going to Europe (for instance Saudis crossing the border to wage jihad in Iraq), are less Westernised and more socially integrated than those active in the West. But they experience the same deterriorialisation process.

The fringe can also be geographic: there are very few Arabs from the Middle East among the second generation of Al-Qaeda activists operating on an international scale (the first generation, that of Bin Laden, went to Afghanistan between 1984 and 1992, generally directly from Middle Eastern countries). Certainly there are a few Syrians (e.g. Imad Eddin Yarkas, known as Abu Dahdah, one of the leaders of the Madrid cell, who lived in Spain and is married to a Spanish national), Jordanians and Iraqis. The Moroccans and second-generation Pakistanis in Europe are over-represented (Moroccans include Abdelkrim Mejjati, Mohammed Bouyeri, Zacarias Moussaoui and Jamal Zougam). More baffling is the number of individuals of East African origin (the authors of the failed transport attacks on London on 21 July 2005), not to mention the converts. In short, Al-Qaeda's recruitment map in no way reflects the flashpoints in the Middle East.

When Mohammed Bouyeri assassinated film-maker Theo Van Gogh in Amsterdam in November 2004, the message he left made no mention of the presence of Dutch troops in Afghanistan and Iraq, but only Van Gogh's "blasphemy" with regard to Islam.

Above all, in nearly all the Al-Qaeda and affiliated cells operating outside of the Middle East there are a large number of converts who often occupy key positions (which is a unique case in the annals of radical Islamic movements). From 10 to 25% of activists are converts.[2] Today, Al-Qaeda's spokesman in Pakistan is an American, Adam

---

2   8% is Robert Leiken's figure, "*Bearers of Global Jihad*", Nixon Center, 2006, but if one includes African Americans (many of whom are converts), it is at least 10%; 25% relates to the Beghal network.

Yahiye Gadahn, whose real name is Adam Pearlman and who hails from California. A certain number of African-American converts are also found in pro-Al-Qaeda networks in the United States, for example James Ujaama, while in in London, among the four terrorists who perpetrated the July 7 2005 underground attacks, was Germaine Lindsay, of Jamaican origin. Another convert of Jamaican descent, Andrew Rowe, who was arrested on board the Eurostar and later jailed for fifteen years on terrorism charges in September 2005, is believed to have associated with another well-known convert in Malaysia, the Frenchman Lionel Dumont. Again in London, Eisa al-Hindi (whose real name is Dhiren Barot), a Kenyan-born British citizen and former Hindu, went to Afghanistan and then to Malaysia, where he married. He was tried and found guilty of plotting to attack financial targets in New York—the whole of Al-Qaeda is on this path. Lastly, another convert was among those arrested in London in August 2006, accused of conspiring to destroy commercial airliners flying to the United States.

In the Netherlands, the so-called Hofstad group, to which Theo Van Gogh's murderer, Mohammed Bouyeri, belonged, was made up of several converts, among them Jason Walters, the son of a black American officer and a Dutch woman (Jason was nicknamed Abu Mujahid Amriki, for the converts often take the name of their country of origin). It was this murder that "shattered" Dutch multiculturalism, even though the group was clearly "post-culturalist".

I also referred to the role of converts in *Globalised Islam*, among them the Frenchmen Christophe Caze, Jean-Marc Grandvisir and Jérôme Courtailler. Many converts are of Caribbean origin (both French and British): they find in Islamist circles a fraternity free from racism and are also motivated by the urge to fight the former colonial power. Here traditional anti-imperialism merges with Islamism. And finally, within Al-Qaeda they achieve positions of responsibility that they would not have access to elsewhere.

The Europeans in Al-Qaeda tend to take one of two routes to conversion: there are those who have pursued a personal path and converted in a mosque, and those who followed their "friends", often into a life of petty crime. A remarkable case is that of the Belgian Muriel Degauque (who carried out a suicide bombing in Iraq with her husband in 2005), for it signals a recent development: the arrival of a generation of women in Al-Qaeda, which until recently tended to be misogynistic in outlook (this reveals how converts also bring with them other forms of deculturation).

There are more converts in Al-Qaeda operating in the West than there are individuals of Middle Eastern origin in the strict sense (i.e. excluding North Africa). This high proportion of converts, beyond all comparison with any other Islamic organisation, indicates several things:

— Al-Qaeda is well and truly a deterritorialised organisation, which in no way expresses a traditional Middle Eastern culture or is a reaction to the Israeli-Palestinian conflict;

— Al-Qaeda recruits individuals who thirty years ago would probably have joined far-left groups (or far-right ones);

— there is a frequent link between petty crime (drugs) and radicalisation, just as far-left movements also had their delinquent tendencies (for example the trajectory of someone like Pierre Goldman).[3]

Al-Qaeda is not a centralised, hierarchical Leninist-type organisation. It operates through networks. These networks are both international and based on close personal relationships between its members who reconcile globalisation and the *esprit de corps* of a small, uniform group of people who know each other well. It is this solidarity between internationalist veterans who have been to the same camps and fought the same battles that gives the networks their flexibility and reliability. And yet, as Marc Sageman has

3 Goldman (1944–1979) was a French left-wing intellectual who was convicted of several robberies and mysteriously murdered.

analysed so incisively,[4] this *esprit de corps* is apparent at the beginning and the end of the initiation journey towards Afghan or another jihad: it is effectively within a small group of "friends" that members become radicalised (on a university campus, in a local neighbourhood, mosque or workplace) and decide to go abroad. In Afghanistan (or Bosnia or Chechnya), they meet other "brothers" who may be Malaysian, Filipino or Pakistani, and whom they may go and visit in their countries. The members of the network often behave in a way that is contrary to what would be expected of an underground organisation. They share apartments and bank accounts, act as witnesses at a friend's wedding, co-sign another member's will, etc. This sense of invulnerability derives from the group effect upon the individual in question, not from the traditional *modus operandi* of a clandestine group.

Al-Qaeda's senior figures, grassroots cells, transnational networks and chain of command are thus rooted in personal bonds, forged either in Afghanistan or at the local level, and which are then transposed to a transnational, "deterritorialised" dimension (exemplified by travel, moving to other countries, multiple nationalities, etc.). Camaraderie

---

4   Marc Sageman, *Understanding Terror Networks*, University of Pennsylvania Press, 2004.

plays a crucial part, sometimes reinforced by marriage ties that have nothing "traditional" about them: members marry a friend's sister but not the woman chosen by their parents, which often implies a relationship between a modern couple, as the wife of Massoud's assassin points out.[5] In the group responsible for the Madrid attack, Serhane Fakhet married his friend Mustapha Maymouni's sister in 2002. In France, Jamel Beghal married Johan Bonte's half-sister.

Al-Qaeda does not confine itself to these networks, for there are others that it draws upon: franchising, branches and lastly the breeding grounds and halfway houses.

— Franchises: it is sufficient for local actors to borrow the Al-Qaeda logo and concept without necessarily being connected to the centre for the organisation to be able to claim responsibility for an action it did not organise. This franchising technique shows to what extent Al-Qaeda is truly a modern organisation: decentralised, flexible, able to delegate, playing on image. The failed attack of 21 July 2005 in London seems to come into this category, whereas the Casablanca attack of 2003, which was thought to have been similar, was in fact linked to the militant Moroccan Islamic Group, connected to the Madrid bombing and to Al-Qaeda. But the flexibility of the possible connection is also illustrated by the Istanbul bombing in 2003: in this instance, the members organised themselves and planned the attack before

---

5   Malika el Aroud, *Les Soldats de Lumière*, ASBL, Les ailes de la misé-
     ricorde, 2003.

making themselves known to Al-Qaeda, which they did during a trip to Afghanistan just before 9/11.

— Branches: local organisations, relatively territorialised (in other words acting within a limited area, corresponding to a country or linguistic region) and with their own history, are instrumentalised by Al-Qaeda and end up explicitly claiming to be affiliated to it. They are to be found in Indonesia (Jemah Islamiyya), in the northern Sahel (the Salafist Group for Preaching and Combat, which in January 2007 changed its name to the Al-Qaeda Organisation in the Islamic Maghreb), in the Sunni triangle of Iraq (the late Abu Musab al-Zarqawi's group) and in Saudi Arabia. These organisations do not need Al-Qaeda in order to recruit or operate. If they have rallied to it, it is precisely because they have difficulty in defining or achieving a local objective (an Islamic state for example); they become globalised therefore by default. Furthermore, members of these organisations have carried out external jihad, where they made personal contacts with Al-Qaeda members such as the Indonesian Ridwan Isamuddin (known as Hambali). The Palestinian activists at the Nahr al-Barid camp in Lebanon, who triggered an armed uprising in summer 2007, belong to this category: second- or even third-generation Palestinian refugees, deprived of any citizenship or hope of returning to Palestine, they are becoming increasingly deterritorialised and disconnected from the struggle to create a Palestinian state.

— The situation in Saudi Arabia is more complex as it seems that there are two either juxtaposed or interpenetrated networks operating: Saudis themselves and foreign volunteers (the Franco-Moroccan Mejjati died at the head of such a group). Young

Westerners have been known to travel overseas to participate in the jihad and then return to Europe to carry out bombings. But these networks can also function in both directions, without there being a clear point of arrival or point of departure.

— Halfway houses and breeding grounds: a particular link is forming between Al-Qaeda and the radical Pakistani networks. The primary reason is that the Al-Qaeda leadership is ensconced in Pakistan (which we have known since late 2001 but was regularly denied by the Pakistani and hushed up by the American authorities). And so it depends on these movements for its protection and to communicate: therefore we are witnessing a Pakistanisation of Al-Qaeda. But on the other hand we are seeing an "Al-Qaida-isation" of Pakistani radicals emerging from the regional area where formerly they were confined (Afghanistan and Kashmir), in particular by linking up with the Pakistani diaspora in Britain (whose radicalisation takes place *in situ* and not under the influence of Pakistan). This tendency is consistent with Pakistan's aspiration to be an ideological, Muslim, state and not a territorialised nation state. For example, one of those accused of involvement in the attempted Heathrow attack in August 2006 is related by marriage to the leader of the Jaishe-Mohammed ("The Army of Muhammad"), an Islamist group long associated with the Lashkar-i Taiba, an armed wing of the fundamentalist movement Dawat ul-Irshad, which is well-established in Pakistan. There are precedents: Omar Shaikh, who murdered the investigative journalist Daniel Pearl, came from Britain, and Willie Brigitte, the French Caribbean convert, was sent to Australia by Lashkar-i Taiba in 2003. Some terrorists in their "born again" phase were members of non-terrorist organisations, like the Tabligh, a pietist movement, but above all the

Hizb ut-Tahrir, which is based in London, and the network that is associated with it, Al Mouhajirun.

Al-Qaeda is therefore developing a two-pronged strategy, involving, above all, spectacular anti-Western attacks, but also the hijacking of local conflicts to bring them under the banner of global jihad. This applied to Bosnia and Chechnya and seems to be happening in Iraq. In these three cases, however, Islamist internationalist groups have been unsuccessful in diverting the local conflict towards other objectives, playing only the role of military vanguard (Bosnia, Chechnya) in a context where the action is taking place solely in a national, territorially defined, space for the time being. The "internationalists", of whatever ilk, then serve as a "Foreign Legion" and move elsewhere once the war ends, as in Bosnia. In Iraq, it is unlikely that the internationalists will succeed in imposing their strategy even if they can play a part in selecting targets (Shia or Christian) and therefore in accentuating the religious dimension of the conflict. It is clear today that all the national liberation movements, whatever the role of Islam (Palestinian Hamas, the Chechens) and whatever their methods, wage their struggle in a national framework, on their territory and on that of those they perceive as the occupying power. No member of Al-Qaeda has acted on Israeli-Palestinian territory and no present-day Palestinian (i.e. one living in Gaza or the Occupied Territories) has taken part in Al-Qaeda actions. But it cannot be ruled out that, faced with international repression and isolation, some groups may decide to internationalise the conflict, as the Palestinians did in the 1970s, by allying themselves this time with the internationalists in the Al-Qaeda sphere of influence. We are likely to see the de-territorialisation of some Palestinians who will abandon the fight for an increasingly unlikely Palestinian state and join Al-Qaeda instead, as happened in the Palestinian camps of Nahr al-Barid and Ayn al-Helwe in Lebanon, and will probably happen in Gaza.

Finally, if ultimately the core of Al-Qaeda is neutralised, it is not too hard to imagine that a certain number of former "Afghans" or potential Al-Qaeda members will market the techniques they have learned, the networks they have built up and their brand image. They could then link up with or transform themselves into mafia networks. They could also serve as mercenaries for state secret services, as did Abu Nidal and Carlos in their day. At present, no state will risk such a move for fear of direct American retaliation. But that could change if the United States attacks Iran, or if there is an internal crisis in Al-Qaeda whereby networks become more autonomous and less politically motivated, or confusion over the purpose and the means of the "war on terror" end up creating a grey area where it is no longer possible to identify the antagonists.

Such a situation may develop in the areas where the internationalist activists are operating today, which presumes links with trafficking networks and the possible complicity of members of the state apparatus (e.g. in the tribal regions of Pakistan).

Is Al-Qaeda playing a key strategic role in the evolution of the conflicts? This remains doubtful. When Al-Qaeda takes over a local conflict, it is never able to impose a new direction on the jihad. Until now, the activists have simply helped escalate a specific conflict, as in Chechnya. In Bosnia, they acted only as a back-up force. In Iraq, the local branch, led by Zarqawi before his death in 2006, played an important role in the radicalisation of the Sunni movement, but above all in combating the Shia, which corresponds to an extant trend. This actually runs counter to the directives of Al-Qaeda, which would prefer armed action to focus on the Americans and their allies. Al-Qaeda condemned Hamas for having chosen the parliamentary route, but it has no influence over the Palestinians. The fact is, Al-Qaeda plays a role in the exacerbation of conflicts, but fails to coordinate them. Local, national, tribal or sectarian religious allegiances are more durable.

Confronted with the intensification of the growing conflict between Shia and Sunnis, Al-Qaeda will have to make choices. The leadership would prefer an alliance with Shia Iran against the Americans rather than to join, as Zarqawi did in Iraq, a Sunni anti-Shia rather than anti-American or anti-Zionist axis. In this case, Al-Qaeda will end up at odds with a whole swathe of its potential recruits, where hatred of Shi'ism remains very strong, as well as finding itself trailing behind events on the ground, unless it returns to carrying out spectacular attacks in order to restore its vanguard image. The fact remains that the activism is increasingly detached from actual political developments.

Al-Qaeda is well and truly part of the *asymmetrical strategy* referred to earlier. Its aim is not to create a new political and territorial entity capable of standing up to the United States, since such an entity would not be a problem for the Americans who would make short work of it, as they did with Iraq in 2001. The purpose is, on the contrary, to increase the "grey areas", where there is no state, no administration, no fixed goals. Al-Qaeda is a nomadic organisation which finds temporary sanctuaries but is able to move on at any time. This is not a return to old guerrilla techniques, brilliantly implemented by General Giap in Indochina and then in Vietnam. For Giap, Mao and their disciples, it was indeed a question at one point of making one area a sanctuary and then moving on to capture another, in short, to acquire the status of the enemy: a territorial sovereign state equipped with an army. Al-Qaeda's battlefield is not that of a conventional army, and here we touch on a major error on the part of the Americans in 2001: namely their decision to opt for the conquest of territory. Al-Qaeda has no political response either, unlike the national liberation movements of the 20th century. True, the utopia may subsequently have turned into a nightmare, but the guerrillas of the past were fighting for a vision of society, and that is something today's jihadists do not have. There is no rosy future for Al-Qaeda, and this void is not unrelated to suicide bombing. The bombers kill themselves from personal ambition, not for a shared vision. We must stop seeing the world through the prism of Al-Qaeda, for that is where its only true strength lies.

The vision of a Muslim world united under the banner of Islam and storming the West makes no sense. On the contrary, what we are witnessing, at least for now, is an increased presence of Western troops in the Muslim world (from Afghanistan to Lebanon and Iraq), conflicts which primarily pit Muslims against Muslims, and lastly a grow-ing gulf between Shia and Sunnis, depriving Iran of the privilege of appearing as the vanguard of the refusal front against Israel and the West, and profoundly altering the alliances and flashpoints in the Middle East, which is more divided and debilitated than ever.

INDEX

Abbas, Mahmoud 56
Abu Nidal 143, 156
Afghanistan 2, 11, 39, 43, 52,
    64, 68, 89, 92, 95, 96-7,
    99, 101, 102, 103, 118,
    139, 145, 150-1, 152
Ahmadinejad, Mahmoud 62,
    73, 117, 120, 123, 124-36
AIPAC 23
AK 57, 62
Al Jazeera 37
Al Qaeda 2, 10, 11, 15,
    25, 52, 54-6, 58, 74,
    115, 118-19, 141-59
Alawites 102, 103-4, 109
Ali, Imam 100, 109
Algeria 61, 62, 68, 83, 90
Amara, Fadela 67
anti-imperialism 5, 136-7, 148
Aoun, General 59, 74, 108
Arab Human Develop-
    ment Report 30

Arab nationalism 8, 44-5,
    85-7, 93-7, 116, 119-20
Arafat, Yasser 96
Assad, Bashar al- 9, 56,
Azerbaijan 105-6
al-Azhar 99
Azzam, Abdullah 96

Ba'ath 78, 85, 91
Baghdad 113
Baha'i 131
Bahrain 105, 107, 109
Baker, James 17; Baker
    Foundation 17; Baker
    report 48, 139
Baku-Ceyhan pipeline 19
Baluchis, Baluchistan
    89-90, 119
Barzani, Massoud 110-11
Bassijis 128-9, 134
Beheshti, Ayatollah Seyyed
    Mohammed Hosseini 131

Belgium 148
Benyettou, Farid 144
Bin Laden, Osama 1,
    15-16, 51, 145
Bosnia 68, 154, 156
Boutin, Christine 67
Bouyeri, Mohammed 146, 147
Bremer, Paul 29, 38
Brigitte, Willie 148, 154
Britain 43, 55, 68-9, 75-7, 141-
    2, 144, 145, 147, 150, 153
broadcasting 37
Bush, George W. 3, 12-13, 17,
    21, 22-3, 49, 53, 121, 122-3

caliphate 75, 100
Casablanca bomb attacks 152
Catholic Church 66-7
Central Asia 19, 35, 37
Chalabi, Ahmed 41
Chechnya 68, 143, 144,
    154, 155, 156
Cheney, Dick 3, 14
Chirac, Jacques 5, 56
Chraibi, Hakil 145
Christians 5-6, 59, 66-7,
    74, 78, 107, 108
CIA 20
civil society 31, 36-8, 41
«clash of civilisations»
    theory 30, 34, 50-1, 87

Clinton, Bill 14, 22-3
Coalition Provisional
    Authority (Iraq) 38
communism 36, 39, 95
Conseil Français du Culte
    Musulman 70
converts involved in ter-
    rorist acts 146-9
Copts 91

Dawa party 104, 120
Dawat ul-Irshad 154
democracy, democratisation
    29, 32, 33-48, 49, 59, 61
Denmark 70
Djerba bomb attack 148
Dyala 113

Egypt 25, 35-6, 38, 60, 61, 62,
    78, 84, 91, 93, 100, 122
Erdogan, Tayyip 51, 57, 59
Ethiopia 2, 84, 146
Exxon 18

Fadlallah, Sheikh 99, 104
Faisal I, King of Iraq 77
Fallaci, Oriana 65
Falluja 47, 86
Fatah 59, 82
Fergany, Nader 30
Fillon, François 66

FIS 83
FLN 83
Ford Foundation 34, 35
France 4, 7, 39n, 49, 55,
    60, 61, 66-7, 68, 70,
    76, 94, 144, 145, 148
fundamentalism/neofunda-
    mentalism 51-2, 56-61

Gaddafi, Col. Muammar 91
Ganji, Akbar 133
Garaudy, Roger 137
gas 19
Gaza 45, 155
Ghalibaf, Mohammed
    Bagher 135-6
Ghilzai 101
GIA 68
globalisation 6, 54, 87, 88-90
Greater Middle East (GME)
    idea 33-48, 84, 90
Greenspan, Alan 19
Gulf states 83-4, 89, 116, 117
Gulf War (1991) 14, 18, 28, 83

Hadhramaut 89
Hama 93
Hamas 2, 26, 45, 48, 49,
    56, 59, 79, 82, 94, 120,
    138, 139, 155, 157
Hariri, Rafiq 56

Hashemites 76-7
Hezbollah 2, 25, 26, 56,
    59, 74, 75, 79, 81, 82-
    3, 90, 104, 108, 117,
    119, 120, 138, 139
Hindi, Eisa al- (Dhiran
    Barot) 147
Hizb-ut-Tahrir 85n, 154
Hojjatiyeh Society 131
Holocaust denial 117, 123, 137
Huntington, Samuel and
    « clash of civilisations »
    theory 30, 34, 50-1, 87

Ibn Khaldun Center
    (Cairo) 35-6
Ibrahim, Saad-eddin 38
India 19, 84,101, 102, 122
Indonesia 89, 97, 152
Iran 2, 18, 19, 21, 24-6, 55, 62,
    64, 73-4, 75, 79, 83, 84-5,
    95-6, 99, 100-7, 111, 116-
    20, 121-40, 157; nuclear
    programme 116, 121-6, 132
Iran-Iraq war 80, 83, 84-6,
    104, 106, 117, 130, 134
Iraq 2, 37, 39-40, 41, 43, 45,
    60, 62, 70, 73, 75, 76, 77,
    78, 84-6, 99, 102, 109-16,
    122, 140, 144, 148, 152,
    154, 156-7; US invasion

and occupation 3-5, 8-9,
   12-21, 23-4, 27-9, 47-8, 84,
   108, 118, 119-20, 138-9
Islam 5-8, 42-7, 48-52, 56-87,
   91-120, 130-3, 144; Islam
   in Europe 51-2, 65-71, 97,
   144-52; see also fundamen-
   talism/neofundamentalism;
   Islamism; pan-Islamism;
   Salafism; Shia Mus-
   lims; Sunni Muslims
Islamism 4-8, 24, 25, 41-2, 43-
   4, 48, 49-52, 56-63, 72, 94
Israel 16, 21-7, 32, 39,
   54, 55, 56, 74, 75, 77,
   78-9, 96, 103, 116,
   122, 126, 137, 139
Israeli-Palestinian conflict
   6-8, 14, 22-7, 40, 67-8,
   75, 81, 82, 94, 109, 110,
   117, 140, 143, 155
Istanbul bomb attack 152

Jaish-e-Mohammed 154
Jannati, Ayatollah 132
Jawad, Mohammed 134
Jemah Islamiyya 152
Jordan 25, 77, 83, 84,
   85n, 94, 109

Karachi 89

Karbala 100, 102
Karzai, Hamid 107
Kashmir 84, 92, 153
Khamenei, Ayatollah (Supreme
   Leader, Iran) 104, 124,
   128, 131, 133, 134, 136
Khatami, Muhammad 126, 128
Khomeini, Ayatollah
   64, 85, 99, 128
Kirkuk 111, 113
Kissinger, Henry 32
Kouchner, Bernard 4
Kurds, Kurdistan 60,
   80-1, 110-15, 133
Kuwait 19, 83, 94, 105, 107

Larijani, Ali 134
Lashkar-i Taiba 154
Lebanon 2, 22, 23, 25, 56,
   59, 77, 81, 82-3, 88, 90,
   99, 102, 104, 107, 108,
   120, 138, 152, 155
Lewis, Bernard 32
Libya 83, 91
Likud 22
Locke, John 34
London bomb attacks
   141, 144, 147
Lyons 66

MacShane, Denis 49

Madrid bomb attacks
145-6, 151, 152
Malaysia 97, 108, 147
Maronites 59, 74, 88, 108
Massoud, Commander 107, 151
Mejjati, Abdelkrim 146, 153
Meridor, Dan 24n
Morocco 46, 62, 70, 90,
146, 152, 153
Mosul 76, 111, 113
Mughals 101
al Muhajirun 154
Murawiec, Laurent 17
Musharraf, Pervez 9
Muslim Brotherhood 51,
52, 74, 78, 83, 85,
92-7, 99, 104, 120

Nahr al-Barid 152, 155
Najaf 101, 102, 115
Nasrallah, Sheikh 117
Nasser, Gamal Abd-al
55, 85, 91, 93, 94
neoconservatives 3-4, 14-
16, 17, 23-4, 27-32
neofundamentalism/funda-
mentalism 51-2, 56-61
Netanyahu, Benyamin 22
Netherlands 70, 146, 147-8
NGOs 33, 36
Nicaragua 55

Nineveh 112
Non-Proliferation Treaty 122
Norton, Augustine Richard 34

oil 16, 17-21, 42
Oman 109
Omar, Mullah 1
OPEC 18
Oslo Accords 14, 22, 25, 45, 78
Ottoman Empire 75-
6, 79-80, 101

Pakistan 9, 60, 69, 74, 84,
86, 89-90, 92, 97, 99,
105, 107, 119, 122, 139,
144, 146-7, 153-4, 156
Palestine 22-7, 44-5, 49,
52, 56, 59, 62, 67-9,
78-9, 81, 84, 92, 144,
152-3, 155, 157
pan-Arabism 23, 77-9,
81, 86-7, 91-7
pan-Islamism 81, 85, 91-7, 116
Pasdarans (Iran Revolutionary Guards) 127-30
Pearl, Richard 154
Pipes, Daniel 17, 48
PKK 111
PLO 96
privatisation 31, 38-9

Project for the New
    American Century 22
Pushtuns 89

Qaradawi, Sheikh Yu-
    suf al- 51, 120
Qom 131
Quetta 119
Qutb, Sayyed 96-7, 141

Rafsanjani, Ali Akbar
    123, 124, 126, 134
Ramadan, Tariq 46, 51
Rauf, Rachid 153
Reagan, Ronald 40, 55
Refah 62
refugees 78, 84
Rumsfeld, Donald 3, 14

Sadat, Anwar al- 55, 78, 93
Saddam Hussein 12-16, 28,
    47, 85, 95, 109-10, 138
Sadr, Moqtada al- 115, 123
Sadr, Musa 102
Safavids 101
Salafism 23, 58, 66, 85-6, 87,
    92-7, 107, 119-20, 144
Salafist Group for Preach-
    ing and Combat 152
Samareh, Mojtaba
    Hashemi 134

Saudi Arabia 14, 17, 20,
    25, 58, 64, 74, 76-7,
    88, 92, 93-4, 95-6, 107,
    118, 122, 152, 153
Schwartz, Stephen 17
Seistan 119
Sepah-i Saheban 105
September 11 attacks
    1, 11-15, 71
sharia 43, 59, 62, 63-
    5, 88-9, 92
Sharon, Ariel 24
Sheykh, Omar 154
Shia Muslims 2, 8, 23, 45,
    60, 74, 75, 79, 80, 88,
    90, 92, 95-115, 117-
    20, 130-3, 156, 157
Shirazi, Ayatollah 105
Sistani, Ayatollah 45, 104
Somalia 2, 43, 84
Spain 70, 90, 145-6, 151
Stewart-Whyte, Don 147
Sunni Muslims 8, 23, 47, 59,
    60, 74, 75, 79-82, 85-6,
    92-4, 98-101, 105-20, 157
Syria 9, 25, 56, 61, 74, 78,
    82, 88, 93, 102, 103-4,
    107, 138-9, 139, 145

Tabligh 58, 154
Talabani, Jalal 111

Taliban 2-3, 11, 43, 58, 59, 60, 64, 74, 119, 139
Tehran 129, 135
Tell Afar 112-13
terrorism 1-2, 9, 10, 13, 16, 30-1, 46, 49, 52, 53-6, 122, 138, 141-59
third-worldism 5, 32
tribes 42-4, 88-91, 102
Tudeh 137
Tunisia 61, 94, 148
Turkey 19, 57, 59, 62, 75-6, 79-80, 111, 122
Turkmens 112

UNDP 30
United Arab Republic 78
United Nations 11, 123, 127, 132
universities 38-9
USA 1-48, 53-4, 86, 116, 119-20, 122-4, 127, 133, 137-9, 142, 146-7, 156, 157-8
USSR 25, 35, 40, 89, 92, 95

Van Gogh, Theo 146, 147-8
Wahhabism 58, 95, 97, 107, 120
« war on terrorism » 12-16, 46, 48, 55, 140, 158
Western Sahara 90
Wolfensohn, James 34
Wolfowitz, Paul 14, 15n, 34
women's issues 35, 65, 148-9
Woolsey, James 20
World Bank 34
World Islamic League 95

Yacine, Nadia 46
Yazdi, Ayatollah Mohammed Taqi Mesbah 131-2
Yazidis 112
Yemen 88, 89, 94, 100, 107

Zarqawi, Abu Musab al- 119, 152, 156, 157
Zawahiri, Ayman al- 59
Zaydis 107